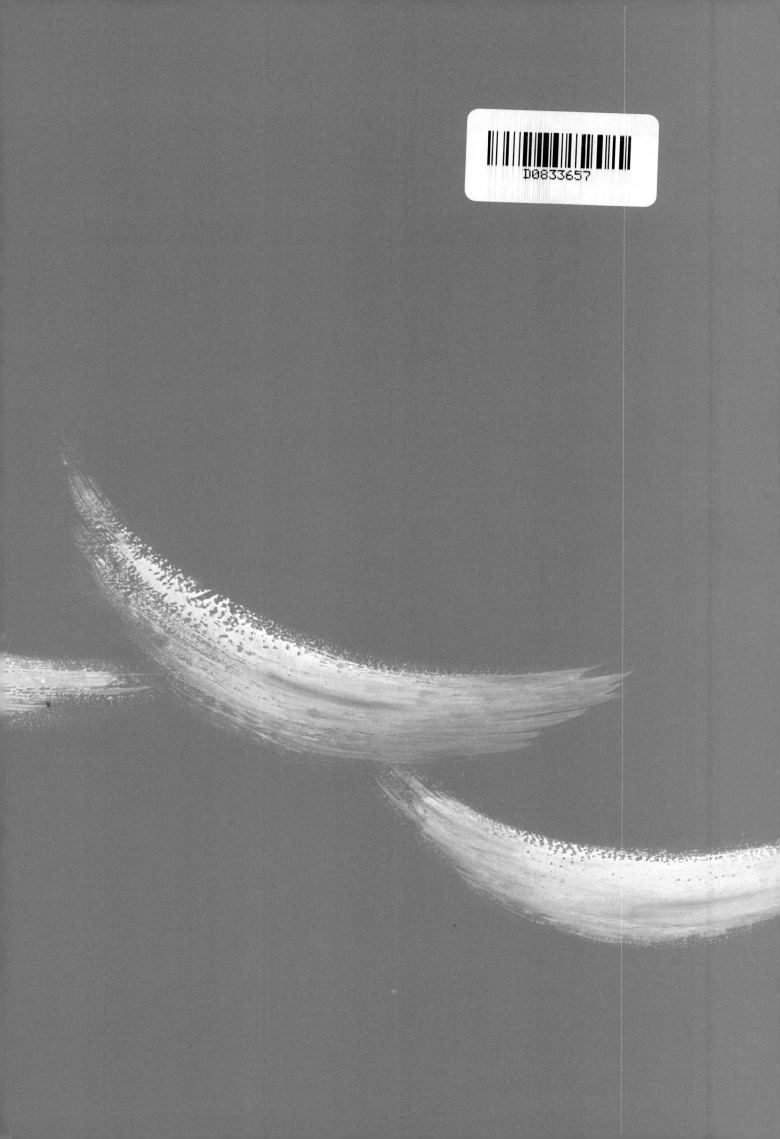

BIRDS OF THE WORLD

This edition first published 1972
Art © 1968, 1971 by Shufunotomo, Tokyo
Text © 1972 Wm. Collins Sons & Co. Ltd.
Published by Wm. Collins Sons & Co. Ltd.
Printed in Belgium by Casterman S.A., Tournai
ISBN 0 00 106189 5

Illustrated by
Takeo Ishida

Text by
DAVID STEPHEN

BIRDS OF THE WORLD

COLLINS LONDON and GLASGOW

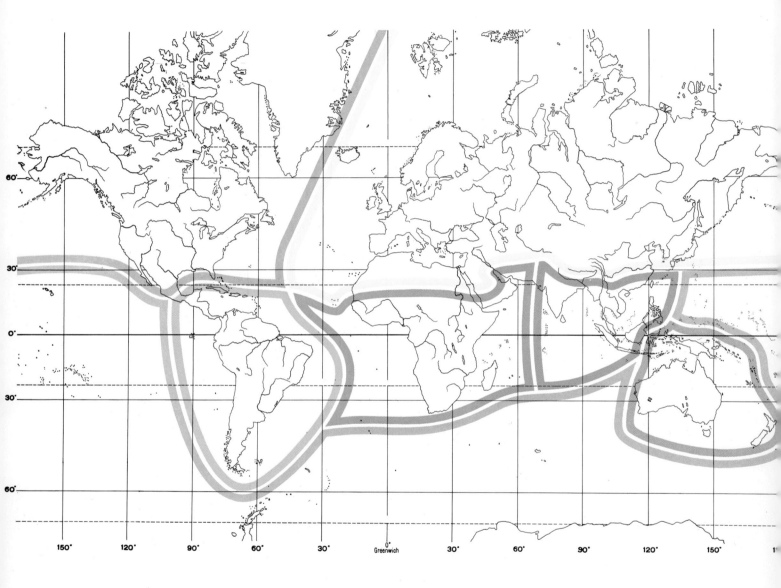

PALEARCTIC

ORIENTAL

ETHIOPIAN

OCEANIC

NEOARCTIC

NEOTROPICAL

AUSTRALASIAN

4

Preface

Birds are distinguished from all other creatures by one characteristic: their bodies are covered with feathers.

The most ancient bird fossils known date from 150 million years ago. The descendants of these populated the various continents and oceans and, to survive, adapted and took on successive modifications imposed on them by the different conditions they met.

In time, therefore, an appreciable number of species diversified. Today there are around 8,500, classified and grouped in 27 orders and 155 families. Classification allows for greater and greater subdivision, and the scientific name finally given to the bird rules out the possibility of confusion.

The zones of the world, shown on the map, are more or less determined by natural barriers, such as oceans, deserts and temperature. Each zone has been colonised by animals and plants, often interdependent. So each zone has its appropriate flora and fauna. Several species can, of course, inhabit more than one zone; and some even have world-wide distribution.

1 Purple Heron

This species breeds in many parts of Europe and southern Asia, as well as in many parts of Africa. To the British Isles, it is a rare vagrant. Unlike other herons, it usually breeds in reed beds and marshes. Less frequently, it nests in low bushes or trees.

2 Great White Egret

The great white egret is a widespread species, being found in south east Europe, Madagascar, New Zealand, North and South America. It frequents reedy swamps, lakes and river deltas, and breeds in colonies in reed beds. To the British Isles it is an extremely rare vagrant. This egret is notable for the flowing nuptial plumes on its back. It is a member of the heron family, and one of the only two white species, the other being the little egret.

3 Little Egret

The little egret is found in marshes, lagoons and flood plains, in parts of Europe, Asia, Australia, Africa and Madagascar. It is a small, graceful heron, with pure white plumage. Its beak and legs are black, but its toes are yellow. Like the larger egret, it also has nuptial plumes, and the birds used to be killed in large numbers when feathers were the fashion. For some reason the plumes were known as osprey plumes.

4 Black-crowned Night Heron

This is another heron with a wide range, being found in North America, Europe, Africa, and in such places as Hawaii and Tierra del Fuego. The night heron nests mainly in trees, but also in bushes, and sometimes in reed beds. Birds breeding in the northern hemisphere migrate southwards after the nesting season.

5 Spoonbill

The spoonbill breeds in Europe and into Russia. It is especially common in Holland. It used to breed in parts of England, but has long been extinct except as a visitor. To Scotland it is a rare vagrant, but it has been observed in the Outer Hebrides and the Shetland Islands.

6 Common Heron

The common heron is found in Europe, Asia and Africa. It is a well known British bird which nests in colonies in tall trees. It is an early nester, eggs often being laid early in February. Young herons are fed by regurgitation. Nesting colonies vary in size from place to place. In severe winters, many herons die. Consequently, colonies suffer a reduction in numbers, and small colonies may disappear altogether. The heron is a fisher, catching perch, sticklebacks, pike, minnows, trout and a variety of other fish. It also takes frogs, small mammals and insects. At times, it even eats other birds.

7 Common Snipe

The common snipe has a long straight bill which it uses for probing into mud to extract the small soil animals on which it feeds. This species is notable for its display of "drumming" in the spring. The male bird swoops in flight and produces the sound with his outer tail feathers.

8 Ruff

The ruff has special display grounds where males gather in spring. Each male has his own stand on which he displays. Females visit the males on the display ground. Ruffs used to breed in England in some numbers, but are now rare.

9 Woodcock

Like the snipe, the woodcock has a special display flight in spring. The male bird flies round his territory at tree height, at dusk, croaking and chirping as he makes his circuit. This display flight is called "roding". There is sometimes a shorter roding flight in the early morning. Woodcocks sometimes carry their chicks in flight.

White Stork

The white stork is found in many parts of Europe, Asia and north Africa, and is well known for its habit of nesting on buildings, from the smallest to the tallest. In some parts it also nests in trees, in groups like the rook. It will nest in baskets placed on the tops of poles.

Like the rook, the white stork adds to its nest year after year. As a result many nests become bulky. The bird lays from 3–5 eggs, which take over 4 weeks to hatch. Both parents feed the chicks, by regurgitation. The young are still looked after by the old birds for a few weeks after they have made their first flight.

White storks eat frogs, lizards, newts, fish of various kinds, and insects. Occasionally they will prey on small mammals. They prey heavily on locusts wherever they find them. This is mostly in winter, when the birds are in winter quarters.

In Britain the white stork is known only as a wanderer. It does not breed. There is said to have been a nest on St. Giles, Edinburgh in 1416. Storks from Europe migrate to Arabia and Africa. Asiatic storks winter in India and the coast of N.E. Asia.

White storks are large birds, measuring more than 3 feet from the tip of the beak to the tip of the tail.

Mute Swan

In most of Britain the mute swan is a semi-domesticated bird, breeding on almost any patch of water, in close proximity to people and dwellings. In the western islands of Scotland it breeds in a truly wild state. In parts of England, where it is a royal bird, it will breed in colonies.

The mute swan is found all over northern Europe and in Russia. It has been introduced to America and Australia. Wild migrants occur in Europe, Asia and the eastern Mediterranean. The mute swan is rarely seen in Spain, Italy, France, Finland or Norway.

This swan has an orange bill, with a black knob at the base. The male is known as the cob; the female is the pen. The species in the semi-domestic state is a notably aggressive bird, driving off other swans from the nesting area, and even other species. Some pens will attack anything in sight, even man. Baby swans are known as cygnets.

10

Whooper Swan

The whooper is at once distinguished from the mute by its black-tipped yellow bill. It is the same size, 5 feet. The whooper swims with its neck almost straight, unlike the graceful S-curve of the mute's.

This swan is found in Europe and Asia. A few pairs breed in Scotland, but to most of Britain the whooper is a winter visitor. It breeds on islets on lakes, or in swamps. The nest is built of swamp plants and moss. The female sits on the nest; the male stands guard close by.

11

Pintail

The long, pointed tail of the pintail drake is his distinctive feature. The duck is like any other brown, speckled duck, not unlike the mallard. Pintails are shy and wary. When the drake is alarmed he will lower his long tail; at other times he often carries it at an upward angle.

Pintails nest in Scotland, but not in great numbers. In England they hardly ever do so. There they are better known as winter visitors. European pintails migrate to southern Africa; birds from Asia go to the Indian Ocean and Japan.

Shoveler

The shoveler is unmistakable because of its large, broad bill. It breeds in bogs, reedy lakes, and other damp places with plenty of cover. It prefers shallow, muddy waters for feeding. The duck makes her nest in open spaces with surrounding cover – on grassland or heath, among reeds or gorse, close to the water.

Smew

In Britain the smew is an irregular and uncommon winter visitor. It breeds in many parts of Europe, in Asia, Africa and east to India and Japan. The drake smew is an outstanding bird in any company, being mainly white. The duck is quite different, with brown head and white cheeks.

Goosander

The goosander is one of the saw-bill ducks, so called because of the sharp saw-toothed edges of the beak. The main prey is fish, including young salmon, trout and perch. Even pike are taken. Most of the fish are small, but the goosander can kill fish of between 8 inches and a foot in length. Goosanders are much persecuted by fishery owners.

Found in many parts of Europe and Asia, the goosander winters from the Baltic Sea down to the Mediterranean. In the breeding season it is found on clean lakes and rivers, mostly in wooded country.

Indian spot-billed duck

The Indian spot-billed duck is found in India and Ceylon. Duck and drake have yellow-tipped beaks; the drake has two orange-red spots at the base of his bill, which the ducks don't usually have. Spotbills are strong ducks, inclined to be aggressive. In captivity they interbreed quite freely with other mallards.

This species isn't such a strong flyer as the common mallard which it resembles in most other ways. The duck makes her nest on the ground, close to the water. The breeding season is from May to December.

Mallard

The mallard is the common wild duck, and often called simply the wild duck. It is the ancestor of most of the domestic breeds of duck, and often reared, like the pheasant, to be released for sport. Wild mallard drakes will interbreed quite freely with domestic ducks. The mallard will breed almost anywhere with enough water, from big lakes and rivers, to small streams and pools. It will breed in public parks, where it soon settles and becomes semi-tame. The duck lays from eight to twelve eggs, and sits for 4 weeks. The drake takes no share. Breeding begins in March. Protected birds will often breed twice in the year.

Teal

The teal is a small duck, not much more than half the size of the mallard. The drake is shown here. The duck makes her nest on dry ground, often far from water – among heather, gorse or bracken. The breeding season is late April into May. The duck lays from 8–10 eggs, and sits for three weeks. The drake helps in rearing the ducklings, but not with the incubation of the eggs. The teal is found from Europe to China, and winters in the Mediterranean, Africa and India.

Mandarin Duck

The mandarin duck is native to Japan, north China, Manchuria and south-east Siberia. It was introduced to England in the 18th century, and at various times later. It bred at the London Zoo in 1834, and has since become acclimatised and well established in many parts of England. It breeds readily enough in captivity, being satisfied with the minimum of water and space.

The drake mandarin, in breeding plumage is perhaps the handsomest of the ducks, and one of the handsomest of birds. Once he has moulted and gone into "eclipse" he closely resembles the duck, but his plumage remains glossier. He keeps his red bill, which distinguishes him at this time.

Mandarin drakes have a social display, after the manner of blackcocks. But they do no real fighting. Their posturing is a ritual. A collection of mandarin drakes on display is one of the great sights in nature.

This is a forest duck, like the American Carolina. It breeds in hollow trees. Captive birds are given barrels, or hollow logs to nest in. The duck lays up to 12 eggs, and sits on them for 4 weeks or a little over.

Because of extensive forest felling in Manchuria and China the Mandarin's existence there is seriously threatened.

Golden Eagle

The golden eagle is found in Europe, Asia and parts of North America. In Britain it is found only in the highlands, islands, and southern uplands of Scotland. Over much of its range it is in decline; but in Scotland it is holding its numbers.

This is a dark brown eagle, almost black, with a wing-span of 6 feet 9 inches to 7 feet 2 inches. Its legs are feathered down to its talons, which are bright yellow. The claws are black.

Prey varies widely – from voles to deer calves. The bird takes what is there. It can kill red deer calves, roe deer fawns and foxes, but the usual prey range is smaller – hares, rabbits, ptarmigan, grouse. In certain areas lambs are sometimes taken. Once in a while an eagle will lift a domestic cat or a small terrier.

Mountain country is the eagle's home. Each pair holds a well defined territory. Most eyries (nests) are at around 2000 feet. Most are built on crags; some are in old birch or pine trees. Two eggs are usual, but often one of them doesn't hatch. Where two chicks hatch one sometimes kills the other. This is most likely where prey is scarce, and one chick becomes dominant.

Nesting begins in March. The young hatch in late April or early May, and fly when about $11\frac{1}{2}$ weeks old. If food is short they will take longer. The eaglets are looked after by the parents until late in the year. When self-supporting they are driven out of the parental territory.

In Britain the golden eagle is specially protected by law, and it is an offence to disturb nests or visit them without a licence.

14

Goshawk

The goshawk is a big, powerful hawk, a two-times sparrowhawk. Being so much bigger than the sparrowhawk, it takes much bigger prey, and is able to kill fox cubs and wild kittens, as well as hares, rabbits, rats, mice and squirrels. It takes a great variety of birds, large and small, from capercaillies and crows to hawks and owls, and down to the size of robins. Like the buzzard it will even, at times, take small nestlings from the nest. It also eats insects and snails.

It is a bold, fast marauder, a specialist at the surprise attack, determined in the pursuit, combining speed with great manoeuvrability and dexterity. With its broad wings and long tail – characteristics of hawks, but not of falcons – the gos is designed for the sudden lift and sharp turn, for threading its way at high speed round trees in the forest, for the sudden check and change of course.

When hunting the gos will either wait on until something appears, or fly around looking for prey. When the prey is sighted the bird attacks with great drive and ferocity, either snatching it in the first strike or flying it down in a long glide. It kills with its powerful feet. It will eat its prey on the ground or in a disused nest in a tree. When feeding on the ground it chooses a quiet spot giving a good field of view. It is not easily surprised on the ground.

Like the sparrowhawk the gos builds her own nest, although she may use the old one of a crow or other bird as a foundation. The male bird helps little at this stage. The nest is built of sticks and twigs, with some greenery added. The female lays three or four eggs, and the young hatch in 36–38 days. At first the male brings all the food, and the female feeds the young. After about three weeks the female brings food too. By then the young are able to tear up prey for themselves.

The goshawk is a forest hawk, with no particular preference for any kind of tree. It is commonly found in coniferous forests; just as readily in mixed woodland; or in woodland of broad-leaved trees. Mostly it roosts in trees, but sometimes it spends the night on the ground on forested plains.

Shooting men on the continent are not usually well disposed towards the goshawk, because it takes as prey some of the species they hunt. This is a narrow view. It is most unlikely that the predation of the goshawk affects their sport in any significant way. Falconers, on the other hand, admire the goshawk for its courage and direct, powerful action. In this sense the gos is in the same category as the peregrine falcon; admired by falconers, looked upon with hostility by many shooting men.

The goshawk is found in Europe and Asia. In America there is a closely related species. It is a rare vagrant to Britain, although there have been breeding records in recent years. The birds were probably falconers' escapes, or birds freed by them. The gos used to breed in the Spey Valley in Scotland.

Sparrowhawk

The sparrowhawk kills mainly small birds which it attacks by surprise. When hunting a hedgerow, it will cross quickly from one side to the other to surprise any small birds feeding on the ground. The female sparrowhawk is much bigger than her mate and can kill prey up to the size of a wood pigeon. The sparrowhen builds her own nest in a high tree. The nest is always built against the main stem. The larch is the favourite tree. The oak is also used as a nesting tree.

Peregrine Falcon

The peregrine is a muscular, powerful falcon, once described as the fastest bird for its bulk that flies. The female is larger and even more powerful than the male. She is properly known as the falcon; the male is the tiercel.

This falcon has a wide prey range – from tiny birds up to species like red grouse, blackcock and large gulls. It kills pigeons, jackdaws, rooks, other hawks, a variety of ducks, and will even attack wounded geese. Sometimes it takes domestic fowls. The peregrine kills mostly by a strike from above, coming down on its prey in a head-long stoop at tremendous speed. Sometimes it will fly a prey straight down or snatch one from its roost. Some peregrines will bind on to a big prey in mid air, holding on with their claws after striking.

Marsh Harrier

The marsh harrier, as its name implies, lives and breeds in marshy areas, swamps and reed beds. The hen makes her nest of water plants and reeds, with a mixture of alder and willow branches. Nests are sometimes of great size. The cock bird makes a small nest of his own.

Like other harriers, the marsh has long

wings, long legs and a long tail. Flight is like that of the others and the bird hunts its territory by quartering the ground with great precision. When a prey is spotted, the bird pounces and snatches. The marsh harrier characteristically flies low over reed tops, flapping and gliding.

Marsh harriers kill a variety of prey – mammals, birds, reptiles and amphibians. They also take eggs and nestlings of other marsh birds.

A few pairs of marsh harriers breed in S.E. England. They are rare wanderers to other parts of the British Isles. They breed over most of Europe, north to Finland and east to Siberia.

Capercaillie

The capercaillie is the biggest grouse in the world the male being almost a yard long. He is a large, powerful bird, bulky as an eagle, with a prominent beard of feathers and metallic plumage of brown, green and purple. The hen is much smaller, and has chequered plumage of buff, white and black.

Capercaillies prefer coniferous woodlands, and their main food is the leading shoots of pine trees. They also eat larch and spruce shoots. This is their main diet from autumn until spring. During the summer months, the birds eat wild berries, seeds, leaves, and grass.

The hen capercaillie nests in the forest, usually on a slope, and almost always near the base of a tree or stump. The nest is a hollow lined with leaves. The cock bird takes no share in incubating the eggs.

In spring, the male birds have a specialised display. They assemble at a traditional site about 3 or 4 a.m., and strut around with their heads erect and their tails spread. During this display, they utter a clicking sound which is ridiculously feeble, considering the size of the bird.

Wood Pigeon

The wood pigeon is one of the best known and widespread of all the wild pigeons. It is found from Norway and Sweden to north Africa, and eastwards to Siberia and the Black Sea.

This species is also known as the ring-dove because of the white patches on the sides of its neck.

It nests usually in trees at a fair height above ground, but sometimes in low shrubs like rhododendrons, within 4 feet of the ground. The usual clutch is 2 eggs, but the bird will rear 2 or 3 broods in a season.

Young wood pigeons are fed by regurgitation. They push their beaks into the parent's throat, and the parent pumps up the contents of its crop for them. Initially, the food is a thick fluid, popularly known as 'pigeon's milk.' Both adults feed the young. Wood pigeons consume large quantities of corn, and so are not liked by farmers.

Hoopoe

This striking bird is found in Africa, Europe and Asia. A few appear in England each spring, passing through. Occasionally, birds remain to nest in the southern counties of England. In Scotland, the hoopoe occurs from time to time in autumn.

More often than not, the hoopoe makes no nest at all. When she does, she is likely to use rags, straw and feathers. The nest is usually in a hole in a tree or wall, but sometimes the bird will use nesting boxes. It likes cultivated areas of orchards, olive groves and woodland. The main food is insect larvae, but it also takes insects such as spiders and centipedes.

Kingfisher

The brilliance of the kingfisher's plumage makes it an unmistakable bird. It is small, being no more than $6\frac{1}{2}$ inches long, including its beak of $1\frac{3}{4}$ inches. The bill is strong and dagger shaped, adapted for catching fish. The kingfisher's upper-plumage is brilliant cobalt, changing to emerald, depending on the intensity and direction of the sunlight. Its under parts are bright chestnut in colour; the feet bright red.

Kingfishers live by the waterside, feed in the water, and nest beside the water. They must have unpolluted water, whether streams, canals or lakes. They eat a variety of fish – minnows, sticklebacks and gudgeon. They take other species of fish, including small trout, the last infrequently. They also eat some insect food, such as large water beetles. At times, the birds will take frogs, tadpoles and newts.

The kingfisher makes her nest in a steep bank overlooking the water. The eggs are laid at the end of a tunnel, up to 3 feet long, which the kingfishers drill out with their beaks. The tunnel is enlarged at the end, and here the female kingfisher lays her eggs. Initially, there is no actual nest. This is later formed of fish bones deposited round the eggs. The entrance to the kingfisher's

burrow is very like that of the sand martin, but sand martins nest in colonies, whereas kingfishers are found in pairs.

The eggs of the kingfisher are glossy and pure white. The usual clutch is 6 or 7. Both sexes share in the incubation of the eggs which hatch in about 3 weeks. Both parents feed the young.

Eagle Owl

This is a giant owl, measuring up to 28 inches in length. It is a powerful bird, with flaming orange eyes and a fierce expression. As with other birds of prey, the female is larger than the male.

Eagle owls breed in Norway, Sweden, Finland, north Russia and in southern and eastern Europe. Related races are found in Africa, Manchuria, China and Japan. In France, the eagle owl is known as the Grand Duc. It is strictly nocturnal, and nowhere common, as it requires a large territory. It frequents mountain forests, open rocky country and barren steppes. It feeds on a variety of prey, both mammals and birds. It can kill birds up to the size of a capercaillie, and mammals up to the size of the brown hare. It has been said to be able to kill roe deer.

Short-eared Owl

This owl (below right) is an inhabitant of open country grass and heather moors, marshes and sand-dunes. It catches its prey on the ground and nests on the ground. Where its territory is partly forest, it may be seen perching in trees during the nesting season.

The main food of the short-eared owl is the short-tailed vole, although it takes birds of many kinds, and mice, shrews and baby rabbits. Where voles become numerous, as in young coniferous plantations, short-eared owls will flock in to nest, so that where there was a pair of owls one year, there could be twenty pairs the next. So long as the voles last, the owls remain. When the voles become scarce, all the immigrant owls depart.

The nest of the short-eared owl is no more than a scrape in the ground, lined with a few bits of grass. The usual number of eggs is from 4–7 or 8, but when short-tailed voles reach plague numbers, the birds may lay up to 14.

Barn Owl

This species is the one most closely associated with man, and is found nesting in farm buildings, dove-cots and church towers. It also nests in holes in trees. It feeds mainly on small mammals, such as voles and mice, water voles and young rats, but it takes some small birds as well. The barn owl begins to hunt just before dusk, when it is often seen as a white shape, drifting along a wood side. The species has become much scarcer in recent years. Where it is well established, it will sometimes rear two broods in a season.

Tawny Owl

The tawny owl (above right) is noted for its long-drawn-out bubbling hoot which is the male bird's salute before he begins hunting at dusk. This species is found in woods and other well-timbered areas, often on the edge of towns. It nests in hollow trees or in the old nests of other birds, such as a crow, magpie and sparrowhawk. It breeds once a year, rearing from 3–5 young. The tawny owl can be extremely aggressive during the nesting period. Then, it is liable to strike at any person intruding too closely after dusk. Some tawnies will do this even when their young are in the branches and able to fly.

European Nightjar

The European nightjar is a swallow-like bird that hunts at night. It is found in woodlands, on ferny hillsides, and in gorse brakes. It has a loud *churring* call, thus drawing immediate attention to itself. Like the swallow, the nightjar feeds on insects which it catches on the wing. It has a great wide mouth like a frog, with bristles along the edges.

Nightjars nest on the ground, among ferns or dead wood. The usual clutch of eggs is 2. When the bird is sitting on her eggs, she is difficult to see because her colour matches her background. When resting in a tree, the nightjar sits along the branch, not across it.

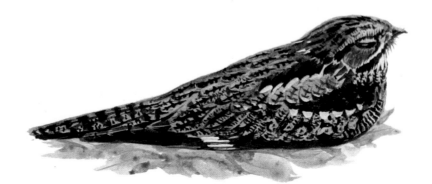

European Cuckoo

The cuckoo is a parasite. She lays her eggs in the nest of other birds, like reed warblers, sedge warblers, meadow pipits and wagtails. A hen cuckoo working a territory will lay up to twelve eggs in a season, so she requires twelve foster parents. She watches the nests on her territory and may destroy the eggs if they are too far advanced to suit her purpose.

The young cuckoo hatches in about $12\frac{1}{2}$ days which means that it is often born before the eggs of the fosterer have hatched. But whether it is born into a nest with eggs or small chicks, it ejects them, heaving them out with its back and using its stump of wings to give itself leverage.

The young cuckoo seems to lose the urge to eject after it is about 4 days old. In the few cases where 2 young cuckoos hatch in the same nest, they spend this period of 4 days trying to evict each other.

24

1 Blackbird

The blackbird is found in Europe, north Africa and parts of Asia. The male is black, with an orange bill. The female is sooty brown, with dark spots on her breast, and a dark bill. Blackbirds are common garden birds, nesting in bushes, trees, ivy-covered walls and hedgerows. They are found also in woodlands and orchards. The cock blackbird is notable for his loud, clear flute-like song which is often delivered at dusk.

2 Song Thrush

The song thrush is also known as the throstle or mavis. It is a common bird of woodlands in Europe and Asia. This species finishes off its nest with a "plaster" lining, of mud, wood pulp and animal dung. It eats much the same food as the blackbird, but is notable for its ability to smash the shells of snails. The bird chooses a suitable rock and batters the snail against it. Such a stone is known as the thrush's anvil.

3 Common Starling

The common starling of Europe is also found in central Asia. It has been introduced to North America and Australia, and has successfully settled in both countries. Flocks of starlings form great roosts in winter, some-times in cities, where they have become a problem, notably in Birmingham, Glasgow, London and New York. In the countryside, the starling is no problem at all. It nests in holes in walls, and rears 2 or 3 broods in a season.

4 Robin

British robins are much tamer than those of the continent, a fact that has been noted by many observ-ers. In Britain, the robin is a common garden bird, and, in winter, will visit kitchens as well as bird tables. It is easily persuaded to come to a window to be fed. In Britain, it is almost impossible to picnic in the country, at any season, without having a visit from the local robin.

5 Nightingale

The nightingale is noted for its song which is powerful and clear, with a great variety of notes. It is also notable for singing after dusk, when other birds are silent. Many poets have written about the nightingale. It is a migrant to Britain, where it nests mainly in the southern part of England. There is only one nesting record for Scotland. Nightingales nesting in Europe spend the winter south of the Sahara.

Great Spotted Woodpecker

The great spotted woodpecker is found in Europe, north Africa and Asia. In Britain, it is widely distributed, frequenting coniferous woodland, mixed woodland and deciduous woodland.

Woodpeckers are so called because they peck wood, using their powerful beaks to drill nesting holes in trees. In the case of the great spotted woodpecker, the nesting hole is almost a foot deep and over 5 inches wide at the base. The entrance to the nest is about $2\frac{3}{8}$ inches high and $2\frac{1}{16}$ inches wide, so it is a vertical ellipse. The site of the nesting hole, usually about ten feet, or a little more, from the ground, is betrayed by the wood chips scattered underneath the tree.

The woodpecker prefers dead, diseased, or dying trees to nest in. Its eggs are white and glossy. The usual number is from 4 to 7. Both birds sit on the eggs, although the hen does most of the work. The young are fully grown in about 3 weeks. They are noisy when well grown, and draw attention to the nesting tree by their calls for food. The main food of the woodpecker consists of the larva of wood-boring insects, but it takes many other things besides. Woodpeckers will even raid other birds' nests. In season, they eat a wide variety of wild nuts and fruits.

Tree Creeper

The tree creeper is a small mouse-like bird that climbs up, down and around tree trunks, in its search for insects. Tree creepers usually nest behind loose bark on tree trunks, or in crevices concealed by moss or lichens. In winter, the bird sleeps in such places, sometimes becoming completely snowed over. Individual birds have been observed scooping out sleeping cavities in the soft bark of Wellingtonias.

The tree creeper makes its nest of moss, grass roots and twigs, and lines it with feathers and wool. The eggs, numbering from 3 to 6, are white with brown spots. The young birds hatch in about a fortnight, and fly a fortnight later. Two broods are reared in a season.

Nuthatch

Like the tree creeper, the nuthatch is a climber. Unlike the tree creeper, it does not use its tail as a prop. It explores tree trunks in short bursts, moving up, round and down with the greatest of ease. Although it finds most of its food on tree trunks, it can also be seen feeding on the ground. It will come to garden bird tables for nuts.

When opening hazel nuts and acorns, the nuthatch wedges them in bark crevices and stabs them with its beak.

The nuthatch breeds in holes in tree trunks or branches. It will use nesting boxes. It adds a collar of mud to tree holes to reduce the size of the entrance. The nesting cavity is lined with pine needles or oak leaves.

Wryneck

The wryneck is often called the cuckoo's mate because it arrives in its summer quarters about the same time. It breeds over much of Europe and Asia. In the British Isles, it is an uncommon summer resident in England and Wales.

The plumage of the wryneck is mottled and streaked like that of the nightjar, but the bird is actually a relative of the woodpeckers. It is extremely shy, wary, and secretive, not often seen, and easily missed. Its shrill cry betrays its presence.

Wrynecks nest in holes in trees or banks, sometimes in the disused burrow of a sand martin, or in a hole in a wall. There is, in fact, no nest as such. The bird lays its eggs on whatever material happens to be lying at the bottom of the hole. Big clutches are the rule – up to ten eggs being common.

Swift

The swift bears a striking similarity to the swallow, but belongs to quite a different family. It is easily confused with the swallow, but can be distinguished by its extremely long narrow wings, shaped like a scythe, and by its short tail and overall dark brown colour. The only part of the swift that is not sooty brown is its throat, which is greyish-white.

Swifts are extremely fast flyers, much given to mounting to great heights. It was long thought that they slept on the wing during the night, and it is now known that birds do stay up for the whole night, coming down at sunrise. Swifts certainly spend most of their life on the wing.

Swifts breed gregariously. In the British Isles, most nests are under the eaves of houses or in holes under the thatch. Some birds nest in cliffs, others will use the old nests of house martins. The breeding season is in June. Only one brood is reared in a season.

In the British Isles, the swift is widely distributed. It breeds throughout Europe, eastwards to Siberia, and southwards to the Mediterranean and north west Africa.

House Martin

The house martin is closely associated with man; hence its name. Most birds nest under the eaves of houses or in out-buildings, usually side by side so that the nests are like a row of houses. The birds return to the same site year after year, patching up old nests or building new ones.

Both birds work at building the nest, which is like a half cup stuck under the eaves against the wall. There is a narrow entrance hole at the top. The nest is built of mud with little pieces of straw mixed into it. The birds carry all the building material in their beaks. The nest is lined with feathers and straw.

House martins breed from late May until the autumn, rearing two broods, and sometimes three. In October, the birds migrate to spend the winter in South Africa or India.

Yellow Wagtail

The yellow wagtail is a bird of water meadows and low-lying fields. Its colour immediately distinguishes it from the pied wagtail which is black and white. It might easily be confused with the grey wagtail which also has a yellow breast, but the grey has a much longer tail.

The yellow wagtail breeds in many parts of Europe and spends the winter in tropical west Africa. British birds arrive in April and May. The yellow wagtail builds its nest on low-lying ground with plenty of cover. The nest is made of bents and reeds, with a lining of hair and a few feathers. Usually the hen does most of the incubating, but both sexes feed the chicks. Two broods are reared in a season.

Great Grey Shrike

The great grey shrike is a member of a family known as butcher birds because of their habit of gathering prey into a "larder". The "larder" consists of dead or living prey which may be wedged in the fork of a tree or spiked on a thorn or barbed wire. The shrike will use the same bush as a "larder" throughout the nesting period, but the habit is not confined to the breeding season.

The great grey shrike is a large bird, $9\frac{1}{2}$ inches long, and able to kill birds up to the size of a fieldfare. It also kills field mice, frogs, lizards and slow-worms. The great grey shrike ranges across Europe to Siberia, and from Norway and Sweden to the Mediterranean. It nests in trees or bushes. The nest is a bulky structure, built of grass and moss on a foundation of tougher material, such as heather. The young shrikes are fed by both parents. Only one brood is reared in a season.

Waxwing

The waxwing derives its name from the bright red waxy tips on some of its wing feathers. In the breeding season, it is confined to the northern forests of pine, spruce and birch. It prefers to nest in younger trees. The nest is built of twigs, moss and grass, with a lining of hair or feathers. Only one brood is reared in a season. Waxwings migrate to many parts of Europe, and are known in Britain only as winter visitors. In some years, there are great invasions of waxwings; in others, the birds are scarce. In Britain, they feed on a variety of berries. They often gather in gardens where there are cotoneasters and other berry-bearing shrubs.

Wren

The wren is a tiny, round-bodied bird with a short upright tail. Although it is not a shy bird, it likes plenty of ground cover from which it makes forays during its search for food. It is an active little bird, hunting leaf litter, tree trunks, boulders, old walls or any place where food is likely to be found. The male wren builds a number of nests, one of which is finally selected by the hen. When she has chosen the one she wants, she lines it with moss or grass or dead leaves or whatever happens to be handy. The nest is a domed structure with a rounded entrance, just large enough to allow the bird out and in. It is lined with feathers. Wren's nests may be found built against the roots of a fallen tree, in crevices in rocks, holes in trees, fern clumps, door hinges, ivy-covered banks or thatched roofs. The female wren sits on the eggs, but the male helps her to rear the family. Two broods are usually reared in a season.

Dipper

The dipper, which is also known as the water ouzel, is an unmistakable bird, with dark brown plumage and a white breast. It is a round-bodied bird, with a short upright tail. It is not unlike the wren, although it is a very much larger bird, being 7 inches in total length.

Clear streams and rivers are the haunt of the dipper, and it is most common in mountainous regions. Typically, it flies low over the water, following the windings of river or stream. Where there is a sharp bend, it may "cut the corner", but usually it prefers to have the river below it. It can often be seen standing on boulders, bobbing and twitching its tail. The dipping movement gives it its name.

The bird is remarkable for its ability to walk into and under the water, where it oars along with its wings, searching the bottom for the water creatures that are its main prey. From time to time, it will bob to the surface, then go down again to continue its hunting.

The dipper nests by the waterside. It builds a large cup-shaped nest of moss and grass which it lines with dead leaves. It builds a projecting roof over the nest, which partly conceals the entrance. The nest is usually built on the face of a rock or cliff overlooking the water, but it may be in a hole in a wall or under a bridge, and sometimes in a tree stump by the waterside. The dipper is an early nester, sometimes laying as early as February. Both parents feed the young which fly in about $3\frac{1}{2}$ weeks. Two broods are usually reared in a season, and some birds may rear a third.

Stonechat

The stonechat (right) is a bird of waste ground, especially gorse brakes and moorland country near the sea. The bird is fond of gorse, and gorse brakes are favourite nesting places. The hen builds her nest either in the bush, or at the bottom of the bush, at ground level. The cock bird can be seen perched on some prominent place while the hen is sitting. Both parents feed the chicks which leave the nest in about a fortnight. Two broods in a season are the rule.

Wheatear

The wheatear (centre) is a common summer visitor to moorlands and mountainous areas of Britain. It is an early arrival and can sometimes be seen when the snow lies deep on the ground. The bird has a distinctive *chacking* call which attracts attention to itself. It breeds in holes in old walls or among rocks or in holes in the ground. The nest is built of grasses or moss, lined with hair, feathers or bits of sheep's wool. Most of the sitting is done by the hen. Both parents feed the young, and the cock will continue to do so if his mate is killed. Where the nest is in an old rabbit warren, the young birds can be seen popping in and out of different burrows.

Pied Flycatcher

The pied flycatcher (left) is found in Europe and Asia. It spends the winter in tropical Africa and parts of Asia. It is a summer visitor to Britain, and breeds regularly in many parts of England. It is not such a common bird in Scotland. This flycatcher breeds in holes in trees or walls, but it will use nest boxes or the old nesting holes of woodpeckers. The main food is insects; hence the name of the bird. But it eats earthworms at times. Unlike the spotted flycatcher, it does not return to the same twig, time after time, after flying out or up to catch an insect.

Great Reed Warbler

The great reed warbler is a large species compared with the reed warbler that breeds in England, being 7½ inches in length compared with 5 inches in the smaller species. The great reed warbler breeds in Europe from the Baltic to the Mediterranean, and eastwards to the Crimea and Syria. It is also found in north west Africa. It winters in tropical Africa and South Africa. As its name indicates, it breeds in reed beds. It frequents similar places in its winter quarters and is also found in papyrus swamps. In the breeding season, several pairs may be found nesting close together. The nest is built around 3 or 4 reed stems, as in the case of the smaller species, and is usually between 2 and 4 feet above the water. The breeding season begins in the middle of May in southern Europe, and progressively later northwards. Great reed warblers rear one brood a year, the young being fed by both parents, and flying at the age of sixteen days.

Blackcap

The blackcap is a warbler, with a considerable variety of calls as well as a pleasing song. The male has a glossy black cap from which he derives his name. The cap of the female is brown. The caps, therefore, distinguish the sexes. Blackcaps like open woodland with plenty of undergrowth. They are also fond of gardens with dense shrubberies. The nest is built in bushes, usually quite near the ground. Favourite places are snowberry bushes, thick hedges and honeysuckle. Both birds share the work of building the nest. The usual clutch is 4 or 5 eggs. Both birds sit on the eggs, and both share in the feeding of the young. The birds feed on insects and wild fruits. Although the blackcap is widely distributed in Europe, Asia and north Africa, it is not a common bird in England, and is even less so in Scotland.

Bullfinch

The British bullfinch (right) is smaller and less brightly coloured than its European relative. Otherwise, they are similar. The stout beak of the bullfinch is adapted for crushing seeds. It feeds to a great extent on buds, berries and seed, including garden fruit, like the gooseberry, currant, apple, plum and pear. This habit has made it unpopular with fruit growers and market gardeners who consider it a pest. At nesting time, the bullfinch feeds its young on insect larvae in the early stages, but very soon they are fed on seeds. Feeding is by regurgitation. To begin with the cock provides all the food. Later, the hen does so too, and the pair can often be seen arriving at the nest together. They perch on the edge of the nest, facing each other, and feed the young together. Bullfinches like thick cover, and are found in gardens, thickets and woodlands. They are fond of breeding in yews, cypresses, box and other evergreens. The nest is usually about 6 feet from the ground. It is built of twigs, moss and lichens, and usually lined with black roots. Some nests are well made; others are loosely built and untidy. Apart from being easily recognised, the bullfinch draws attention to itself by its familiar piping call.

Goldfinch

The goldfinch is a handsome bird, with its crimson face, white cheeks and yellow wing flashes. Although it is widely distributed in Britain, it is absent from many areas, and is a scarce bird in Scotland. In many parts, it is more familiar in wintertime, when flocks move about the country, feeding on the seeds of many weeds. Thistles are a great attraction, and the birds work hard, stripping them of their seed. Birch catkins and alder catkins are other favourite foods. The goldfinch also eats insects, and the young are fed on insects in the early stages. The young are fed by both parents, one at a time. Feeding is by regurgitation. The goldfinch nests in gardens and orchards and similar places. It is particularly fond of nesting in fruit trees. The nest is neat and compact, built of roots, grass, moss, lichens and wool, and lined with down or wool. The hen incubates, and during this period, is fed by her mate. Two broods in the season are the rule.

Great Tit

The great tit is the largest species in this numerous group, and is found in Europe, Asia and north Africa. This species likes mixed woodlands, copses, gardens, orchards and such places. It nests usually in a hole in a tree or wall, but it is just as likely to choose anything from a squirrel's drey to an empty petrol can. It also uses nesting boxes and, where these are provided, it will use them year after year.

Willow Tit

The willow tit is a much smaller bird than the great tit. It nests in holes in trees, but makes the nesting hole itself by boring into rotten wood. It chooses trees like birches, willows and alders. The work of boring the nesting hole is shared by both sexes. The inside of the chamber is usually lined with rabbit wool and wood fibre. The usual clutch of eggs is 8 or 9. Small tits like the willow tit are called chicadees in North America.

Blue Tit

The blue tit is one of the best known of all tits, being common in gardens where it readily uses nesting boxes. In winter, the local birds are joined by wanderers, so that the garden has many more blue tits than in spring or summer. This species is fond of woodlands, hedgerows and thickets and, in such places, nests in holes in trees. But it is notable for using a variety of odd nesting sites – letter boxes, old drain pipes, old cans, and even the nests of other birds, like rooks and crows.

Long-tailed Tit

The long-tailed tit is easily distinguished by its long tail and the flush of pink in its plumage. It is also remarkable for its nest which is built in the open. It is built almost entirely of moss and cobwebs, with a little hair through it. It is large and oval-shaped, and covered completely with lichens. It is lined with feathers and as many as two thousand have been counted in the lining of a single nest. This warm, beautifully constructed, almost weightless nest is built in a thorn bush or gorse bush. Other trees, like blackthorn, oak, birch and spruce, are also used, and sometimes the nest may be as high as fifty feet above the ground.

Golden Oriole

The golden oriole is found over most of Europe and in parts of Asia. It has nested from time to time in several English counties, but is known in Scotland only as a wanderer. Golden orioles winter in tropical Africa, South Africa and Madagascar. In the breeding season, orioles frequent mixed or deciduous woodland and other well timbered places, especially near rivers. The hen oriole builds a remarkable nest. It is built like a hammock, slung under the branch of a tree to which it is strongly laced. It is built of sedges, bark, grass and wool, and lined with the flower heads of various grasses. Like the blackbird, the oriole often adds bits of paper to its nest. The usual clutch is 3 or 4 eggs. The male sits on the eggs for a short spell each afternoon. Both parents feed the young, which fly about a fortnight after hatching.

34

Hooded Crow

The hooded crow is found in northern and central Europe and western Asia. Where its range overlaps that of the carrion crow, the two interbreed freely and the offspring are fertile. The offspring show all the characteristics between the black carrion and the black-and-grey hooded crow. It is now considered that the two are colour phases of one species. The hooded crow eats a great variety of animal food. It is a predator and a scavenger. In Britain, it is not liked by shepherds because it will attack sickly or weak lambs. It raids the nests of many birds, taking eggs or nestlings. The hooded crow builds a strong nest of sticks and twigs, thickly lined with sheep's wool or such material. It prefers to nest in single trees or on the forest edge, so that it has a good view of its surroundings.

Jay

The jay is a small distinctive crow, brightly coloured, with black crown feathers and bright blue on its wings. It is a bird of tall woodland, with plenty of undergrowth. It is shy, alert and wary, usually seen when flying away, when it displays the white patch on its rump. Because of its readiness to sound the alarm at any strange sound or movement, it has been called the "watchdog of the woods". Its harsh cry carries for a great distance. Jays eat all sorts of wild fruits and berries, but also take eggs, young birds, mice, earthworms, insects and other animal food. They are fond of acorns which they hide in the ground, thus planting oak trees. The planting of acorns by jays explains why oak woods can grow uphill.

Magpie

The Magpie is another crow, unmistakable because of its pied plumage and its long tail which glistens green, blue and purple in the sun. Like the jay, the magpie is alert and wary. Magpies nest in woodlands, gardens and hedgerow trees, sometimes in low hedges only a few feet from the ground. The nest is a large structure of sticks and twigs, with a strengthening of earth and roots, roofed over with other sticks in such a way as to leave an opening at the side. Hawthorn is commonly used for the roof of the nest. Magpies display much social activity in the early weeks of the year, when large numbers gather together, posturing and chasing each other, and showing great excitement. After that, the pairs separate to begin nesting.

Japanese Crane

Japanese folklore refers to the long life of the crane, perhaps a thousand years. The species is certainly long-lived, but the actual life span is probably well under a hundred years. Nevertheless, this is a long life compared with most birds, and it compensates for the low reproduction rate – 1 to 3 eggs per nest – and the high mortality among young birds. The Japanese crane has become extremely rare, and is on the danger list of world species. It breeds from eastern Siberia to Japan, but its Japanese breeding strength is now reckoned to be in the region of two hundred birds. The pressure of civilisation on its breeding and wintering grounds is reckoned to be

the main cause of its decline. It winters in China. The Japanese crane is a large white bird, with black wings and a grey face. There are fourteen or fifteen species of cranes in the world, distributed from America to Asia, and south to New Zealand and Polynesia. At least two species are on the verge of extinction. It is thought that all cranes pair for life. All of them have a ceremonial dance, performed mainly in the breeding season, although some species do so throughout the year. Northern cranes are noted for their migrations, when they fly in ''V'' formation, like wild geese.

Indian Peafowl

The Indian peafowl is a native of India and Ceylon. It
has been well known in Europe since the days of
classical Greece and Rome. It was later introduced to
France and England, where it was important as a table
bird until the introduction of the turkey from Mexico
in the fifteenth century. Indian peafowls, however,
still held their own on the large estates where they were
kept and bred as ornamental fowl. They have lost
ground since the first World War, and are now an
uncommon sight outside zoological gardens. Peafowls
are considered sacred in Hindu countries, so they are
unmolested and tame. In other parts of their range,
where they are hunted, they are shy and wary. As
ornamental birds in Europe, they have proved hardy
and easy to keep. They breed freely, and are not aggressive. Many people dislike their harsh cries, but they
are handsome birds and an attraction wherever they
are given freedom.

Malay Great Argus

The Malay great argus is found in Malay, Thailand and
Sumatra. The species is still abundant in its home areas,
but is not so common nowadays in Europe, where it
was once bred in considerable numbers in captivity.

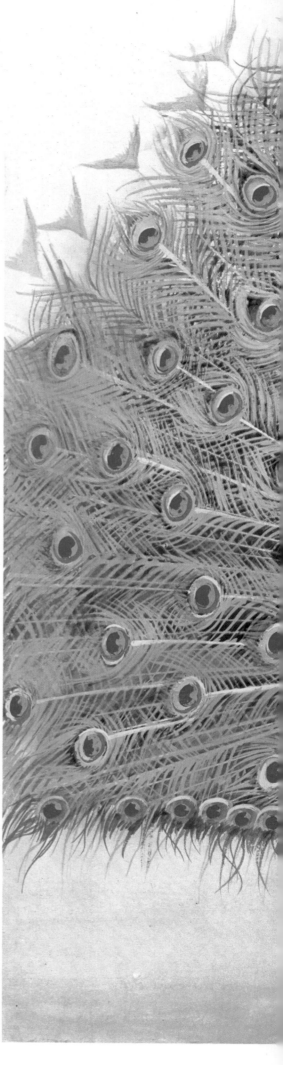

Lady Amherst's Pheasant

The range of Lady Amherst's pheasant is from Tibet to south west China, and south to the borders of Burma. It frequents woodlands and scrub in mountain areas, especially bamboo thickets. The main food is bamboo shoots. This species was first introduced to Britain in 1828 by Lord Amherst. In England, the species was often allowed freedom in parks and coverts, and there was, inevitably, some cross-breeding. Pure-bred birds can still be seen at Woburn Abbey.

Reeve's Pheasant

This species is found in the high plateaux of central and northern China. It is a forest bird, and is common where the forests still stand. When the forests are felled, Reeve's pheasant disappears with the trees. It is usually seen in small flocks, up to six thousand feet. The first cock bird was introduced into England in 1831. A female was brought in 1838. There was some cross-breeding with other pheasants. More birds were subsequently introduced to France and England. In Europe, Reeve's pheasant readily inter-breeds with other species.

Swinhoe's Pheasant

Swinhoe's pheasant (right) comes from Taiwan. It is found nowhere else as a wild bird. On Taiwan, it inhabits mountain forests. It was discovered in 1862 by Swinhoe, an English naturalist, who was Consul there at the time. The bird was introduced to Europe in 1866 and, since then, has become a common bird in captivity. In captivity, Swinhoe's pheasants produced a cinnamon variety which bred true, but all these birds died during the first World War. The type has not reappeared.

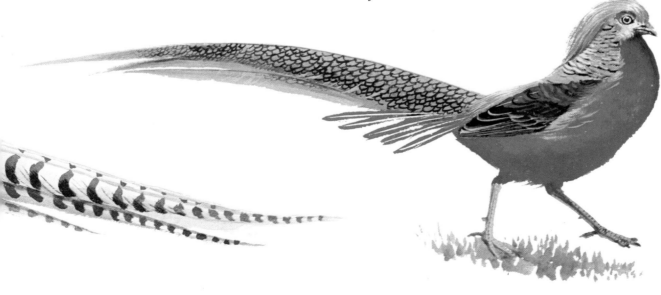

Silver Pheasant

This (top) has always been a popular pheasant in captivity. It is a large bird, completely hardy and tame, and breeds well. Silvers have been familiar birds in Britain since the 18th century. Although tame in captivity, the cock birds are very aggressive towards other species, and sometimes towards human beings. Within their own groups, however, they live amicably, the cocks showing little inclination to fight with each other.

Golden Pheasant

The golden pheasant is a small type, found in the mountains of central China. It has been known in Europe since the 18th century. It has long been a popular bird in Britain and, when given freedom, breeds wild. Under controlled conditions, it crosses readily with Lady Amherst's pheasants. During the incubation period, the golden hen rarely leaves the nest, and just as rarely eats or drinks. Captive birds breed freely, even when enclosed in small areas. The birds are surprisingly hardy. They come on to lay early, and will produce a large number of eggs if they are not allowed to build up a clutch and become broody.

Satyr Tragopan

There are 5 species of tragopan, which are also known as horned pheasants. They are large, stout birds, with a short beak and rounded wings. The satyr tragopan is found in the wooded mountains of the central and eastern Himalayas. In captivity, the bird is demanding in its food requirements. It must have a great variety. It has been known in Britain since 1863. (Below left)

Himalayan Monal

There are 3 species of monals. These are short-legged pheasants, with long bills. The upper mandible is long and adapted for digging. The Himalayan monal is found in the Himalayas up to fifteen thousand feet, and ranges from eastern Afghanistan to southern Tibet. It is still a common bird on its home range, where it frequents open forest of oak, birch and rhododendron. It feeds on a variety of roots, berries, seeds and shoots, and probes actively with its beak when foraging. (Below right)

Ring-necked Pheasant

The ring-necked pheasant (above) belongs to the true pheasants which occur in many types over Asia, especially in China. Ring-necks have been known in Europe since antiquity. When brought together in captivity, or when turned loose as sporting birds, all the types inter-breed freely. Cock ring-necks have a partial white ring on the neck. They are extremely hardy, and breed well in the wild state. It is more customary, however, to rear them in large numbers under artificial conditions, then turn them loose into covert. Even during the war years, the pheasant survived in Britain as a wild bird when there was little, if any, artificial rearing. The hen pheasant likes thick ground cover to nest in. During the laying period, she covers her eggs with withered leaves, or other herbage, until she is ready to brood. In the early days, she takes fright readily and is easily flushed, but as incubation proceeds, she sits more closely and, latterly, will allow herself to be almost trodden upon before taking flight. Some hens will even allow themselves to be stroked on the nest.

Tailor Bird

The tailor birds of south east Asia are well-known garden birds, and there are several species. They have long, straight bills and long tails. Tailor birds are notable for their nest building. The bird chooses a large hanging leaf of a shrub or tree, and sews the edges together with plant fibre.

Baya Weaver Birds

The true weaver birds are confined to Africa south of the Sahara, except for a few species in India and Malaysia. One of the eastern species is the baya weaver which is found in Pakistan, India, Ceylon, Thailand, Indo-China and Sumatra. Weaver birds are notable for their suspended nests which are beautifully woven with vegetable fibres. The style of nest varies from species to species, but they are all woven, and all hang from the branches of trees.

Indian Mynah

The Indian mynah, from the forests of India and the East Indies, is well-known in Europe as a cage bird. It is widely kept because of its powers of mimicry. Hence its other name of talking mynah.

43

Great Hornbill

Hornbills derive their name from their enormous bills. In some species, there is a large casque on top of the bill, which looks heavy but is, in fact, extremely light. The casque varies in shape from one species to another, and is smaller in the female than in the male. The great hornbill of Malaya, found from India to Sumatra, measures fifty-two inches in length. The bill of this species is enormous. Its casque is also of great size. Hornbills are remarkable in another way. The female lays her eggs in a hole in a tree, up to a hundred feet from the ground. Then she walls herself in, plastering the entrance hole with material brought by her mate. She uses dung or clay for her plasterwork, and leaves an entrance hole just large enough for her mate to pass food through to her.

44

Ostrich

The ostrich is the largest living bird. A fully grown adult male stands almost 8 feet tall to the crown of his head, and may weigh up to 3 cwts. Even forgetting the long neck, the bird stands over 4 feet tall at the shoulder. Ostriches are birds of dry plains and semi-desert. In East Africa, they are also found on bush and thorn savanna. In some parts of Africa, large groups of birds can often be seen together. The usual group is a male with 3–5 hens, the males being polygamous. All the females lay their eggs in the same nest, the nest being nothing more than a scrape in the ground. Up to thirty eggs are usual but, in the Masai country, as many as fifty have been found. The male ostrich broods the eggs during the night; the female ostriches take turns by day. Ostrich eggs are a delicacy, and are eaten by men and animals, especially jackals.

Social Weaver

The social weaver is found only in South Africa. This is a sociable species, and the birds build a communal nest. The nests are built in large acacias, and all the birds of the colony, male and female, work at all times to keep a communal roof over the group of nests.

Secretary Bird

The secretary bird is a long-legged predator, found in Africa south of the Sahara. It is a bird of the plains, where it hunts snakes, lizards, small mammals and large insects, running after them at speed, and using its wings for balancing and turning.

45

White Pelican

The white pelican is found in Europe, Africa and Asia. It is found in inland waters, and feeds principally on fish, although it also takes crustaceans. Pelicans often fish in disciplined fashion, quartering the water with their wings flapping. They are strong flyers and, once airborne, can fly at great speed and at a great height. They often fly in formation, after the manner of wild geese. They are colonial nesters, some of them nesting in trees and some of them on the ground. The young pelicans in the nest are tended by both parents. The nestlings push their beaks into the parents' gullet for food – not into the great pouch for which the pelican is famous. Contrary to popular belief, fish are not carried in the pouch.

The Great Flamingo

Flamingos, when adult, are always pink in colour, with bill and legs of red or yellow. They are tropical birds, found at varying altitudes, but always in association with brackish or salt-water lakes. One species lives in the high Andes, inhabiting alkaline lakes at a height of fourteen thousand feet. They obtain their food by turning their bills upside-down. They take water into the beak, then the tongue, acting as a piston expels it 3 or 4 times a second. Stiff outer hairs prevent food from being lost. Food consists mainly of tiny blue-green algae and diatoms. Flamingos breed in colonies, sometimes in large numbers. In Africa, colonies approaching a million can be seen at one time. The greater flamingo breeds in Africa, the Camargue, and in the Persian Gulf area. There are 3 types which are no longer considered as separate species. The nest of the flamingo is usually a cone of mud about a foot high, with a shallow depression on top, which the bird scoops out with its bill. The great flamingo will sometimes breed on rocky islands, and make a nest of grass and feathers. Flamingo eggs are chalky white with a blood-red yolk. When sitting on the nest, the flamingo gathers her legs beneath her. Despite the large number of young in a colony, each bird appears to recognise its own chick.

Marabou Stork

The marabou stork (left) is a large bird, about 4 feet tall, and with a wing span of over 8 feet. It has an extremely heavy, straight bill. On the front of its neck, there is a patch of pink skin which can be distended like a balloon. At times, this pouch is very obvious and striking, but nobody yet knows what its function is. The marabou is an African stork, and a notable scavenger. In fishing villages it scavenges fish. Elsewhere, it scavenges refuse. It also eats small mammals. It is often seen in the company of vultures where a large animal has died, and it is not unusual to see a number of marabous feeding with up to a hundred vultures of several species.

White-backed Vulture

The white-backed vulture (right) of Africa is a gregarious species, and it is not uncommon to find hundreds of them on a large carcass or carcasses. In the breeding season, the birds nest in colonies, always in trees. The nest is a large structure of sticks, lined with leaves. The young vultures remain for a very long time in the nest. The male feeds his mate and young with carrion which he re-gurgitates for them.

Vulturine Guineafowl

The vulturine guineafowl is an African species that frequents semi-desert and bush savanna. For many months of the year, it depends on dew for its water. This is one of the most attractive of all the guineafowls, which are well-known all over Europe as domesticated birds. The domesticated birds are not derived from this species.

Red-billed Dwarf Hornbill

The red-billed dwarf hornbill is a very small African species, measuring only fifteen inches from the tip of its beak to the tip of its tail. Like other hornbills, this species nests in holes in trees, which the female then plasters up, leaving only a slit through which she is fed. The dwarf hornbill female moults quickly after sealing herself in. Once she has renewed her feathers, she breaks out of her prison and helps her mate to feed the young. The young hornbills then re-plaster the entrance, sealing themselves in until they are fully fledged and ready to leave.

Paradise Whydah

The paradise whydah belongs to a group known as widow birds. It is found in Africa south of the Sahara, on savannas and plains, but not in deserts or forested areas. In this species, the 4 central tail feathers are longer than the wing and, of these 4 feathers, the inners are longer than the outers. The male whydah is aggressive during the nesting season, and is thought to be polygamous, but this is still not beyond doubt. Like other species of widow bird, the paradise whydah is a social parasite, laying its eggs in the nests of other African weaver finches. The eggs resemble closely those of the chosen host, and the chicks have mouth markings and plumage like the young of the fosterer. Unlike young cuckoos, however, young whydahs do not evict their foster brothers and sisters from the nest.

Crowned Crane

The crowned crane is found over much of Africa, from Ethiopia and the Sudan southwards. It is found in Kenya, Tanzania, Zambia and Uganda. It is the national emblem of Uganda. The species is notable for its beautiful crown of feathers. Like other cranes, the crowned species likes plains with marshy ground and pools. It spends all its life on the ground, in or out of water. The main food is vegetable matter. Crowned cranes will also eat insects, small mammals, and sometimes small birds.

4 Fulmar Petrel

3 Wandering Albatross

1 Manx Shearwater

5 Wilson's Petrel

2 Pomatorhine Skua

1 Manx Shearwater

The manx shearwater is an Atlantic and Mediterranean species. It breeds in burrows which are excavated by both sexes. Breeding colonies are found as high as three thousand feet in Scotland. The shearwater lays one egg. Both sexes incubate in turn, each bird sitting for several days. The chick is fed once in twenty-four hours, at night, and deserted by its parents when it is 2 months old.

2 Pomatorhine Skua

The pomatorhine skua is an Arctic species which breeds in the tundra. It is not sociable, and nesting pairs are widely scattered. It preys mainly on lemmings, but eats all sorts of carrion. Like other skuas, it is a pirate, forcing other birds to disgorge food.

3 Wandering Albatross

The wandering albatross is one of the heaviest flying birds in the world, the male weighing about 27 lbs. It is pelagic, spending its life, outside the breeding season, at sea. The fledgling period of the young is long – about 5 months.

4 Fulmar Petrel

The fulmar petrel is another pelagic sea bird. It breeds in colonies on turfy cliff-tops, sometimes in easily accessible places. It lays one egg. This species has a habit of regurgitating oil from its crop when too closely approached by an intruder.

5 Wilson's Petrel

Wilson's petrel is another pelagic sea bird. During the breeding season, it resorts to rocky islets, cliffs, and other stoney places in the Antarctic. The nest is usually under a mass of loose rocks, but sometimes in burrows which the birds excavate for themselves. Like the storm petrel, Wilson's also "walks" on the waves.

6 Great Frigate Bird

7 Red-tailed Tropic Bird

10 Great Black-backed Gull

8 Arctic Tern

9 Common Tern

11 Black-headed Gull

6 Great Frigate Bird

The great frigate bird is notable for its nuptial displays, during which the males perch on bushes and inflate their balloon-like throat pouches which are brilliant scarlet in colour. The great frigate bird breeds in colonies and islands in the Indian Ocean, the south Atlantic, and the central Pacific.

7 Red-tailed Tropic Bird

The red-tailed tropic bird of the Atlantic, Pacific and Indian Oceans is notable for its ability to fly momentarily backwards.

8 Arctic Tern

The Arctic tern, which nests in the northern hemisphere, performs spectacular migrations to the southern hemisphere, flying half-way across the world.

9 Common Tern

The common tern, like the Arctic species, breeds in Britain and in the northern hemisphere. It winters in the southern oceans, and on the coasts of the Antarctic Continent. Common terns nest in colonies on sand-dunes, salt marshes, and islands. They are vociferous and demonstrative in defence of their nests and young, and will attack human intruders.

10 Great Black-backed Gull

The great black-backed gull is one of the giants of the gull family, measuring up to 27 inches in overall length. It is a powerful bird, able to kill weakly lambs, as well as a variety of birds and mammals. It is also a considerable carrion eater.

11 Black-headed Gull

The black-headed gull is really a brown-headed gull. The brown hood is worn only in the breeding season. During the winter, the birds have merely a dark mark behind the eye.

1 White Ibis

2 Anhinga

3 Great Blue Heron

4 Roseate Spoonbill

1 White Ibis

The white ibis is distinguished from the herons by its red, curved beak and red legs. This species is found in the southern states of North America, south to Venezuela and Peru. It is sometimes called the white curlew.

2 Anhinga

The anhinga, found in the southern United States, southwards to the Argentine, is popularly known as the snake bird. It is, in fact, one of the darters, and closely resembles the cormorant. Like cormorants, the darters breed in colonies and build huge nests, but unlike cormorants, they nest in trees and build their nests of sticks instead of seaweed.

3 Great Blue Heron

The great blue heron, found from Alaska to the Argentine, including the West Indies and the Galapagos Islands, is the largest and commonest heron of the Americas. It nests in colonies, usually in trees, but sometimes on the ground.

4 Roseate Spoonbill

The roseate spoonbill is the only member of the spoonbill family found in the New World. It is found in South America and the southern states of the United States of America. Like other spoonbills, it breeds in colonies, the nest being built of sticks, in a tree or bush, although some are built among reeds on the ground. The chicks when hatched, have short,

5 Brown Pelican

6 American Purple Gallinule

7 Osprey

8 Limpkin

straight beaks, but quickly develop the length and the special shape that gives the species its name.

5 Brown Pelican

The brown pelican is distinguished from all other pelicans by its dark plumage. It is found in the southern United States on both coasts south to the Galapagos and Chile. It is a marine species that catches fish by diving into the water after the manner of the gannet.

6 American Purple Gallinule

The American purple gallinule is found in the southern United States and South America. It is a species of waterhen, allied to the waterhen or moorhen of the British Isles.

7 Osprey

The osprey of Europe is known in North America as the fish hawk because it preys mainly upon fish. The osprey dives into the water to catch its fish, then flies with its prey held pointing forward in its feet. Ospreys like to nest in tall trees although, in Europe, some birds nest on cliffs. After being extinct in Britain for half a century, the osprey returned to Scotland as a breeding species, and several pairs now nest each year.

8 Limpkin

The limpkin, also known as the wailing bird or crying bird, is a wader, found in swamps and other shady places in tropical America – Georgia, Florida and southwards. The species feeds almost entirely on snails.

1 **North American Canvas back Duck**

2 **Great Northern Diver**

4 **Carolina Duck**

3 **Green-winged Teal**

5 **Pied-billed Grebe**

6 **Canada Goose**

7 **Snow Goose**

1 *North American Canvas back Duck*

The North American canvas back duck is a relative of the pochard, and closely resembles it. It is one of the diving ducks, and a favourite sporting bird in North America.

2 *Great Northern Diver*

The great northern diver breeds in Arctic North America, southward to California and British Columbia. It disperses widely at sea in the wintertime.

3 *Green-winged Teal*

The green-winged teal breeds from the far north of America, south to New Mexico, and spends the winter in the Bahamas and West Indies.

4 *Carolina Duck*

The Carolina duck is notable for its nesting habits. It nests in holes in trees. It breeds readily in captivity, and has been introduced to many European countries.

5 *Pied-billed Grebe*

The pied-billed grebe is widely distributed in North and South America. Some grebes are also known as dab chicks.

6 *Canada Goose* is described on pages 56–57.

7 *Snow Goose*

The snow goose, which is pure white, breeds in Arctic North America and Siberia, nesting in colonies on the tundra.

8 *Killdeer Plover*

The killdeer plover breeds in North America, southward to the Bahamas and Mexico, and winters from British Columbia southward to the Bermudas and Venezuela. Like most birds of the plover family, the killdeer makes a cautious, roundabout approach to its nest. In the breeding season, it is found near ponds and lakes on dry upland pastures.

8 Killdeer Plover

9 North American Golden Plover

10 Turnstone

12 American Bittern

11 American Avocet

13 American Coot

14 Trumpeter Swan

9 North American Golden Plover

The North American golden plover is found on the tundra and Arctic heathlands of North America. It makes spectacular migrations southward to the pampas of South America. This plover builds its nest on the open tundra, laying its eggs in a depression in the moss. The birds leave on their southward migration at the end of July.

10 Turnstone

The turnstone breeds in the Arctic north, and spends the winter as far south as Australia.

11 American Avocet

The American avocet breeds in southern Canada and the northern United States. It spends the winter on the prairies of Central America.

12 American Bittern

The american bittern, like other bitterns, is noted for its booming voice. The booming is a far-carrying sound, and has been rendered phonetically as "klunk er glunk". Like the others too, it is noted for its concealment posture. The bird stands rigid, with its bill pointing to the sky and its feathers pressed close to its body, so that it matches its background of reeds.

13 American Coot

The American coot, like other coots, has a white shield on the front of its head, giving it a bald appearance.

14 Trumpeter Swan

The trumpeter swan is notable for its call. It is now an extremely rare bird in North America, being found in a few parts of Canada and in Yellowstone National Park.

Canada Goose

The Canada goose is a large species, measuring up to 40 inches in overall length, compared with under 3 feet in the grey lag goose. It is greyish-brown in colour, with a black head and neck, but has a striking white patch round its throat which extends upward behind its eyes. This goose breeds in Alaska, Canada and the northern United States. It nests on islands and in marshy areas, usually in colonies, but sometimes only a few pairs may be found together. Although it is mainly a ground nester, it has been known to use the old nest of the osprey, and sometimes to nest on a crag far from water. The nest is a hollow on the ground, lined with dead leaves, reeds and grass, and padded with down and feathers. The Canada is an early nester, breeding at the beginning of April. While the goose is sitting on eggs, the gander stands guard close-by. He plays the part of guardian after the goslings have hatched, but their main care is undertaken by the goose.

The Canada goose was introduced to the British Isles in the 17th century, and was well established as a breeding bird in the 18th century. It is now widely distributed and common, and many Canadas breed in Scotland and England. In Britain, nests are usually on small islands on lakes, and often among young timber.

This species domesticates readily, and can be left as a full winged bird where it has been reared. When brought in as adult, it is usually pinioned until it has become settled.

In Britain, the main food of the Canada goose is grass, although it will also eat a variety of water plants. In America, when on spring migration, it flies down to corn fields to feed. In its Arctic breeding haunts it eats berries as well as grass. It is said also to take a certain amount of insect food and some worms.

The voice of the Canada goose is a loud, resonant honk which is very distinctive and quite unlike the call of the grey lag. Like other geese, the gander has a triumph call when he has driven off an intruder. In the case of the Canada, the triumph call is usually accompanied by snake-like movements of the neck.

Andean Condor

The Andean Condor is a large black bird with some white on its wings. Its head and neck are naked, the colour varying from red to yellow. In the male Andean there is a great mass of fleshy tissue on the crown, looking rather like the rose comb of some male domestic fowls. This species is found in the Andes Mountains of South America, from sea level to altitudes over ten thousand feet. It is the largest of all vultures, with a wing span of almost 10 ft. It nests on cliffs or crags. The young condors are a long time in the nest, up to 11 weeks. As in other vultures, the main prey of the condor is carrion. Its feet are not adapted for killing prey. A related species, the turkey vulture, is known to take eggs and young sea birds.

Californian Condor

The Californian condor is almost as big as the Andean species. It is now an extremely rare bird, and is one of the world's endangered species. A population census between 1939 and 1947 estimated that only about seventy birds remained in the entire mountainous area of California, although, at one time, its range extended into Mexico. The last counts in 1963 and 1966 indicated that in 20 years, the population had fallen by 30 per cent. The decline seems to be continuing, despite legal protection for the condor and every attempt to safeguard its nests from destruction. Hunters are still the main culprits in the bird's decline, although their attitude to it appears to be changing. This condor is a slow breeder. It lays one egg, and doesn't breed until the age of six.

Turkey Vulture

The turkey vulture (left) is often called "John Crow" or turkey buzzard in the United States, where vultures are commonly known as buzzards. Although its main food is carrion, it takes eggs and young sea birds on the Peruvian Islands. This species ranges from Canada south to Tierra del Fuego.

Black Vulture

The black vulture (right) is a common and widespread species, known as the carrion crow in Guiana and the Antilles. This species is about the same size as the European buzzard. It, also, is a carrion eater.

Vultures

Vultures are large birds of prey. Because the head and neck have no feathers the birds look very ugly. Vultures feed on carrion (dead creatures), tearing at the flesh with their strong beaks. Their claws are too weak to cope with living prey. Although they have many characteristics in common, Old World vultures and American vultures are different enough to be classified in separate suborders. The American group includes the Andean condor and the Californian condor shown on pages 58–59.

Golden Eagle of North America

The golden eagle of North America is the same bird as that found in Europe and Asia. In America, it is also a bird of the mountains, nesting on crags and cliffs. In some parts of America, the bird is heavily persecuted, and is even shot on the wing from aircraft. It is disliked by sheep men who are its main persecutors. In parts of Asia, this eagle is trained to fly at wolves, foxes and antelopes. The wild birds take small antelopes and deer, and kill fox cubs.

Red-tailed Hawk

The red-tailed hawk of North and Central America is a bird of coniferous woodland, hardly ever found in treeless regions. It is a member of the buzzard family and, like the common buzzard, is much given to soaring. This species is notable for hovering above mountain ridges, hanging motionless for minutes at a time.

Swallow-tailed Kite

The swallow-tailed kite of North America is white, with black tail, wings and back. Although it bears the same name, it is quite a different bird from the swallow-tailed kite of Africa. It is an elegant, handsome bird, graceful and spectacular in flight. It has been much persecuted, and its numbers become fewer each year.

American Sparrowhawk

The American sparrowhawk is really a falcon, more properly a kestrel, but falcons are commonly known as hawks in North America. The present species is very small, measuring from 9–11 inches in overall length. It is found over most of North and South America. It nests in holes in cliffs, in trees, and in the giant cactus of the desert. American sparrowhawks from the far north of their range migrate southwards; but rarely farther than Mexico and Central America. Not long after the second World War, a bird of this species arrived in Scotland, having fallen exhausted on to a weather ship, 400 miles out in the Atlantic.

Bald Eagle

This white-headed eagle is the United States national emblem, but it is fast becoming a rare bird. It is much persecuted in Alaska, and its numbers have declined in the southern part of its North American breeding range. It is one of the species that has been seriously affected by D.D.T. This poison, by poisoning insects, contaminates the fish that eat the insects and, at the end of the chain, contaminates the fish eagles that eat the fish. The bald eagle is a fish eagle. In addition to D.D.T., contamination of rivers has meant fewer fish and, therefore, destroyed great areas of suitable habitat. Besides fishing for itself, the bald eagle is piratical on the osprey. It chases the osprey and forces it to deliver up its catch. Like the osprey, the bald eagle is often a sociable bird, and 2 or 3 pairs may be found nesting within a mile of each other. They build their large stick nests in the topmost branches of tall trees, up to 120 feet from the ground.

American Whooping Crane

The American whooping crane is in danger of extinction, and is now rigidly protected by law. Its population is now so low that all the present protection efforts may be of no avail, although there has apparently been some slight increase in recent years. In 1963, the wintering population in Texas, which means the world population, was estimated at 33 birds, 7 of which were the young of that year. Aransas in Texas is the wintering place of every whooping crane in the United States. American ornithologists make an annual census of numbers when these birds are migrating from Canada. They are extremly graceful and beautiful birds, and are thought to pair for life.

Sandhill Crane

The sandhill crane of North America and Siberia is becoming a very rare bird. Its population is now estimated at about 170,000. In Florida, it is resident; more northerly populations migrate to Mexico and the southern United States. This species has a bare, bright red patch on its crown.

Willow Grouse

This is a circumpolar species that nests on the tundra of the far north. In the British Isles, it nests only in Scotland, and only on mountains over three thousand feet. The willow grouse changes to white in winter and, at the time of the spring moult, cocks lose their white later than the hens, thus attracting attention to themselves while the hens are sitting. The willow grouse of South America is notable for its fluctuation in numbers. Its cycles match those of the 4-year rodent cycle. The hen lays her eggs in a scrape on the ground, and sits so closely that a person could walk right over her. In Britain the willow grouse is known as the ptarmigan.

Sage Grouse

The illustrations show male and female of this species. In the sage grouse, the plumage of the sexes is not so strikingly different as in birds like black grouse, pheasants or capercaillies. The male of the sage grouse has wattles and air sacks of greenish-yellow colour. Like the black grouse, the sage grouse gathers in spring for ceremonial displays. Its display ground is known as the dancing ground. The sage grouse sometimes performs considerable migratory movements, travelling up to a hundred miles in search of winter feeding. This is a species of semi-desert land, found on the prairies of the American West.

Ruffed Grouse

The ruffed grouse, unlike the black grouse and certain others, does not gather for ceremonial displays. Like the black grouse, the ruffled grouse is a bird of heathland and the scrub areas of the forest fringe. Where forests are felled, it can extend its range on the cleared ground.

Road Runner

The road runner belongs to the family of the ground cuckoos. It is a large, slender bird, up to 2 feet in overall length. It has a long tail and an obvious crest. It has long, strong legs, well adapted for running and, although it can fly, it spends most of its time on the ground. It preys on small ground animals, and is able to kill a rattlesnake. It is found in the western United States, especially in the more southerly parts, where it is known as the chaparral cock, which indicates that it is a bird of semi-desert regions. Although it is a member of the cuckoo family, it builds its own nest and rears its own young.

Bobwhite Quail

The bobwhite quail is the best known of all the American quails, being one of the most popular sporting birds in America. It ranges, in its many forms, from southern Canada to Guatemala. The bobwhite is a bird of the prairies, but it does well also in the cultivated areas of eastern North America. Introductions of this species to Europe have not met with any success. North American quails generally resemble the European species. The bobwhite has no crest, but it can erect the long feathers of its crown at will.

Wild Turkey

The two species of wild turkey, with their several races, are confined to North America, although their domesticated descendants have settled in most parts of the world. The name "turkey" is a misnomer. When the birds were brought to Europe, they were mistaken for guineafowls, and their origin was mistakenly believed to be the east, so the name "turkey" arrived, and has remained. One race of the wild turkey was domesticated by the Puebloes of New Mexico 1400 years ago, and it was known in America as a domestic bird when Columbus arrived. It made its appearance in Britain in the 16th century. The male turkey is noted for his gobbling cry. The domesticated varieties reach great weights. The race originally introduced into Europe was the south Mexican turkey, domesticated by the Indians in Mexico.

Pileated Woodpecker

The pileated woodpecker is found in the coniferous forests of North America. After the nesting season, it moves southward to Central America, where it is usually found in small groups moving about in trees. This is a very large woodpecker, black and white, with a red crest. Like other woodpeckers, it makes its nest in a hole in a tree. The only lining is the sawdust in the bottom. The eggs are white.

Blue Jay

The blue jay is found from southern Canada, south to the Gulf of Mexico. It is a forest bird, with bright blue plumage and white patches on its wings and tail. Like so many of the crow family, the blue jay is omnivorous. When food is plentiful it will carry away the surplus and hide it for use later. This characteristic is most noticeable in more northern areas, although all jays, Old World and New World, have the habit. Like other jays, the blue is a bright, inquisitive bird, making a habit of appearing at camp sites and such places, on the lookout for titbits.

Cactus Wren

The cactus wren is found in dry mountain areas and deserts of south western United States and Mexico. It feeds on insects and larvae which it finds on thorny shrubs and cactuses. Unlike most wrens, it does not skulk among ground cover, but shows itself quite openly. A related species from further north hunts by turning over the ground litter and stones, after the manner of the common blackbird or the turnstone.

Northern Mocking Bird

The northern mocking bird, found from Canada south to Mexico and Jamaica, is well-known for its loud, clear song and its rich variety of notes. It is also an accomplished mimic, copying the songs of other birds, hence its name. But it is such a versatile singer, and so disregards pattern, that it produces a great variety of notes without trying to mimic. Hence its mimicry has been much exaggerated. It is now believed by American ornithologists that about ten per cent of its song represents the true copying of other species.

American Robin

The American robin is a thrush, but received its name because of its red breast. This, one of the favourite American birds, was seriously threatened by D.D.T. which was used to control the elm bark beetle. In one part of the Mid-West, over a million birds died as a result of this kind of spraying. The American robin is a migratory species which winters in Guatemala.

Bluebird

The bluebirds of North America are noted for their song. They are familiar birds in gardens, public parks and woodlands. They belong to the same general group as the nightingale and the robin.

Ruby-crowned Kinglet

The ruby-crowned kinglet is a tiny tit-sized bird that belongs to the same group as the goldcrest and the firecrest. It was once thought to be a member of the tit family, but it is not a tit: nor is it a wren. It is a warbler. There are 2 types of kinglet in North America: the golden-crowned, which is like a firecrest, and the ruby-crowned which has a red crest. The nest of the ruby-crowned kinglet is built of moss and cobwebs and lined with feathers, like the nest of the long-tailed tit. It is beautifully constructed. The bird builds its nest in tree tops, sometimes at a great height. It is suspended from the fine terminal twigs, like the goldcrest's nest.

Cedar Waxwing

The Cedar waxwing is found in the coniferous forests of Canada and the northern United States. Like the waxwings of Scandinavia, it is notable for irregular migrations and irruptions, appearing in more southerly areas in some winters, and not in others. The movements of these birds are so erratic that they are just as likely to turn up in China or Japan as in Europe. The cedar waxwing usually builds its nest in pine trees, but this is not an invariable rule. The nest is built of twigs, lined with moss, grass and feathers. Nesting birds are usually associated in twos or threes but, in wintertime, large flocks are usual.

Magnolia Warbler

The magnolia warbler lives in coniferous forest or mixed forests in Canada and north eastern United States. It winters in Central America. Like other warblers, the magnolias are insectivorous. Recent research in Maine established that a pair of these birds will feed their young a beakful of insects once every 4 minutes.

71

Eastern Meadowlark

The eastern meadowlark of North America belongs to the same family as the cow birds which are promiscuous and parasitical, like cuckoos. The meadowlark is monogamous, and builds its own nest, like the meadow pipit of Europe, in low herbage, well concealed. The bird twists the grass stems over its nest as a further concealment, a characteristic noted in the British redshank which is a wader.

Marsh Blackbird

The marsh-dwelling blackbird of the western prairies of North America builds its nest in reeds or other vegetation a few feet above the water. The nest is an open cup, like that of the common blackbird, and is strongly built. In such a situation, it is out of reach of most ground predators. This handsome species is one of the American orioles. After the nesting season, it moves from its prairie breeding haunts to spend the winter in Mexico.

Scarlet Tanager

In the scarlet tanager, the male's plumage is brilliant scarlet, with black wings and tail. This species migrates to South America in the winter, at which time the males moult to green and yellow, becoming more like the females. This tanager is the only member of the family that changes plumage to such an extent. Like other tanagers, it prefers the tree tops rather than the gloom of the forest floor or understorey. It hunts on the ground, and is mainly a fruit eater. The scarlet species builds an open cup-shaped nest, usually in trees or bushes, sometimes at a great height.

Painted Bunting

The painted bunting is aptly named, and has been described in various ways as the most brilliantly plumaged bird in America. The under-parts of the male are red. His head is blue; his rump is red; he is green on the back. This species is found in the United States and Mexico.

Cardinal

The cardinal belongs to the family of cardinal-gross-beaks, most of which are buntings. It is found in the temperate regions of North America, southwards into Central America, and on some of the islands, and has been introduced into other areas, notably the Bermudas and California. In these areas it has become a pest to fruit growers. The male cardinal is brilliantly coloured; the plumage of the female is much browner.

Snow Bunting

The snow bunting, which has a circumpolar distribution, moves south in winter, and down from the heights where it nests. In winter, it is usually seen in flocks. The North American bird is the same as that found in northern Europe and on the high mountains of Scotland.

White-throated Sparrow

There are many members of the bunting family in North America, among them a large variety of handsome sparrows. One of these is the white-throated sparrow, found in forested areas of Canada and in the north eastern United States. This is a sparrow-sized bird. It nests usually in a bush or tree, not far from the ground, and sometimes quite close to the ground. The nest is cup-shaped. Other American sparrows in tropical areas build dome-shaped nests.

Sabrewing

The sabrewing is confined entirely to Colombia.

Mitchell's Humming Bird

Mitchell's humming bird is found in forest areas near the equator.

Ruby-throated Humming Bird

The ruby-throated humming bird beats its wings about 60 times per second.

White-booted Rackettail

The outer tail feathers of the white-booted rackettail extend like long thin wires, each ending in a "racket".

Humming Birds

Humming birds are mostly extremely tiny some of them no bigger than bumble bees. They are noted for the metallic brilliance of their plumage. They behave like insects, hovering before flowers and sipping nectar with their long beaks. There are more than 300 species of humming birds in the world. The bee humming bird is the smallest of all, its total length being hardly over 2 inches, and half of this is made up of beak and tail. The largest species is the giant humming bird of the Andes, which is over 8 inches in total length. Humming birds have to eat a lot of food each day. In this, they are like shrews which have to eat every few hours, or die. During the day humming birds pay frequent visits to flowers for nectar or, in some cases, to catch tiny insects. During the night, they rest. Some of them fall into a deep sleep resembling hibernation.

Cock of the Rock

The cock of the rock belongs to the cotinga group of birds, and is notable for its social displays resembling the lek of the blackcock. Each male stamps out a place for himself, where he holds frozen postures for minutes at a time. The male cock of the rock is orange-red in colour, with black markings on his wings. He has a helmet of feathers that almost conceals his beak.

Three Wattled Bellbird

The three wattled bellbird has three fleshy snake-like appendages hanging from its beak, one from the top and one from each side. From these, it derives its name.

Quetzal

Quetzals are among the most colourful of birds. They belong to the trogon family which are forest dwellers that nest in tree cavities, and feed mainly on insects and other invertebrates. Some of them also eat berries and fruit. The quetzal is very fond of a fruit that resembles the avocado, and also eats insects, tree frogs, lizards and snails. It takes most of its insect food off the leaves when hovering in front of them.

Umbrella Bird

The umbrella bird is another member of the cotinga group. When the male is displaying, he opens his crest so that it covers his entire head. While doing so, he utters a rumbling sound. But there is no social displaying as in the cock of the rock.

Ara Macaw

This macaw is one of the ara group – a scarlet species, with wings of blue, streaked with yellow. It lives and nests in the forests of Mexico and Bolivia, and the south of Brazil.

Blue and Yellow Macaw

The blue and yellow macaw is found from Panama to the Argentine.

Macaws

Ara macaws are members of the parrot family, found in the rain forests of Central and South America. They are all brilliantly plumaged in contrasting colours. Like other parrots, they are great favourites as cage birds and household pets, because of their intelligence and their sense of attachment. Unfortunately, this has led to a decline in the number of wild macaws, and some species are threatened by over-exploitation. Macaws are found from Mexico to Paraguay. They are the largest parrots in the world, and a fully grown specimen will measure over 3 feet in length, including its tail.

Like other parrots, macaws are excellent climbers, and assist themselves with the beak, using it as an extra foot. All of them are vegetarians in the main, although some species eat insects from time to time. In captivity, macaws eat a wide variety of food, including nuts. All of them can use their foot as a hand when doing so.

Toucans

Toucans inhabit the rain forests of Guiana and Brazil. This is one of the largest species, belonging to the group known as ramphastos. The males are bigger than the females, but the sexes are alike in plumage. Toucans nest in trees, using already decayed cavities. Smaller species will use old woodpecker nesting holes. The larger species remove the rotten wood to make the hole big enough for nesting in. The nest is often at a great height. Both birds incubate the eggs, and both take turns at brooding and feeding the nestlings. The main food consists of fruit and insects, although larger prey is sometimes brought. Some toucans will take the eggs and nestlings of small birds. Others kill snakes and lizards. When the toucan wants to reach fruit at the end of a branch, its long bill is an advantage, enabling it to sit back where its weight is comfortably supported. But it has other uses. It is used to repel enemies and predators.

Flightless Cormorant

This member of the cormorant family has very small wings, and is unable to fly. Despite this, it has the typical cormorant habit of standing on a rock and holding its wings out to dry. In most ways, it behaves like other cormorants. It is not found outside the Galapagos. It is strange that the bird should have evolved towards flightlessness, but this is possibly explained by the total absence of predators. The flightless cormorant has another distinction; it is the largest of all species. Its plumage is dark and it has blue eyes. Although clumsy ashore, it is highly accomplished in the water.

Grosbeak Finch

This grosbeak finch is one of those discovered by Charles Darwin when he visited the Galapagos during the voyage of the *Beagle*. Its heavy beak, which is of great size, is designed for seed eating. All the finches of the Galapagos are highly specialized birds, and important in the study of evolution.

Darwin's Finch

This is another of the Darwin finches, known as *Camarhynchus Pallidus*. It is an insect eater. It is able to use the cactus spine as a tool. It pushes the spine into a hole or crevice which it has already excavated with its beak, and thus prises insects out. There are 4 Galapagos finches that are tool users.

Blue-footed Booby

The blue-footed booby is found from Mexico to Peru and the Galapagos. Like the Peruvian booby it nests in vast colonies. It is a member of the gannet family, and an excellent diver and fisher. It has an inflatable air sack that helps it in resurfacing.

The diet of the blue-footed booby is entirely fish. It derives its uncomplimentary name from the fact that it is so easily captured. It is persecuted by the frigate bird and often has taken away the fish it has caught.

Unlike other gannets, this species lays two eggs. Incubation starts with the first egg so that one chick hatches before the other. The first chick, being stronger than the second, usually manages to secure all the food, so condemning its unfortunate nest mate to starvation and death.

The booby has no feathers on the throat and lower jaw. Unlike other gannets it will breed in trees and bushes.

Kiwi

The kiwi is a flightless New Zealand bird. Why some birds should be flightless is still argued. It is sometimes said that birds develop from two sources: those that could fly, and those that could not. But it is now generally believed that kiwis and other flightless birds evolved to the point of losing the power of flight because they had no longer any need for it. The kiwi is now a rare species. There is considerable variation in the size and weight of kiwis from one species to another. Weight ranges from 3–9 lbs. The females, in all cases, are larger than the males. The usual food consists of earthworms, insects and berries. The egg of the kiwi weighs about a pound, and takes eighty days to hatch.

Emu

The emu (right) is another flightless Australian bird, found in forests and on open plains. In wheat country, it can be a pest. The emu builds her nest under a tree or bush. She lays from 8-10 eggs incubated by the male.

Cassowary

The cassowary is an ostrich-like bird and, like the ostrich, flightless. It is found in Australia and New Guinea. It is a nocturnal species, and shy. But it is aggressive and can be dangerous. In New Guinea there have been several records of human deaths as the result of encounters with cassowaries. The female cassowary lays from 3-6 eggs which are incubated by the male.

Brush Turkey

Brush turkeys are also known as "junglefowls". The present species is confined to the eastern coast of the Australian mainland, although its relatives are found all over the country. Other species are confined to New Guinea. Brush turkeys are birds of tropical rain-forests, but the present species, known as Latham's junglefowl, is also found in drier scrubland. Brush turkeys are shy, elusive birds, not often seen. They like to skulk about in cover, and will not take wing until forced to do so. The birds build nesting mounds about 12 feet in diameter and 3 feet high. These are made of vegetable matter which heats up like damp corn-ricks. The males take charge of the mounds, and will not allow the females to lay their eggs until the temperature has fallen to the proper level. In the early stages of fermentation the temperature is much too high. The males allow cooling air into the mounds by turning over the material.

Mallee Fowl

The mallee fowl, also known as 'lowan', is another junglefowl, found in semi-arid scrubland in Australia. It is most commonly found in the scrub known as 'mallee'. In its arid environment, the mallee fowl has to adopt different arrangements to keep its nesting mound at the proper temperature. In these areas, there is wide variation between day and night temperatures. The birds overcome this obstacle by excavating a hole about 15 feet in diameter and 3 or 4 feet deep. They gather material from a wide area and fill the hole during the winter months. After the material has been moistened by rain, the birds cover it over with a layer of sandy soil, up to 2 feet thick. The buried vegetation, thus sealed, begins to ferment, and soon the necessary heat is generated. The male mallee fowl looks after the mound and, like the brush turkeys, he prevents the temperature from rising by probing into it with his beak and allowing cool air to circulate.

Crowned Pigeon

The crowned pigeon is found in the forests of New Guinea. It is a large pigeon, about the size of a hen brush turkey, and has a vertically flattened crest of lacy feathers. It lives on fruit and grain. Although protected by law, it is much sought after by hunters because of the quality of its flesh.

Black Cockatoo

Cockatoos belong to the family of the parrots, but this group is confined to Australia, Papua and nearby islands. Cockatoos are easily recognizable because of their crests which they can erect at will. The black cockatoo has almost black plumage. It has a powerful beak, hooked like that of a bird of prey, which it uses for crushing and opening nuts. It feeds mainly on the nuts of the palm tree.

White Cockatoo

The white cockatoo is closely related to the parrot and is more of a true cockatoo than the black. It is a very shy bird, found in Australasia and the East Indian islands. It is generally white with tinges of red, orange or pink.

Kookaburra

The kookaburra is found in most parts of Australia, where it is also known as the laughing jackass. It is one of the family of tree kingfishers, most of which live in trees. They catch insect prey in the air, or pounce on prey on the ground. Prey includes reptiles and small birds. The laughing jackass is a large bird, measuring more than 15 inches in length.

Satin Bower Bird

Bower birds are found only in Australia and New Guinea. Some of them are very small, about the size of a crow. Bower birds, as the name suggests, build bowers to attract females. The male strews the ground with coloured objects. The satin bower bird builds his bower early in the season. He collects coloured objects and displays to the female. His displays last for several months, until the season is right for breeding. During this time, he paints his bower, using such things as fruit pulp or charcoal mixed with saliva.

Birds of Paradise

Birds of paradise are found mainly in New Guinea and adjacent islands, but there are a few species in northern Australia and the Molucca Islands. Birds of paradise vary widely in their choice of habitat and food. Some are found on mountains at high altitudes; others are found in forests. Some of them are carnivorous, feeding on lizards and frogs. Some are insect eaters. Others are fruit eaters. The males are the most brilliantly plumaged, but in some species they have no special decorations. Where the males and females are not brightly coloured, the birds are usually found in pairs. The brilliantly coloured males are the ones that display like black-cocks, and like blackcocks, are promiscuous or polygamous. In the species that pair, the male helps to rear the family. In the species where the males are brilliantly coloured, and do not pair, they take no part in rearing the family. The most highly ornamented males are the ones that go in for the most elaborate displays. Some species display singly. Others, like blackcocks, gather on a display ground and perform in company. During such displays, every part of their ornamentation is emphasized. They erect and spread their highly coloured feathers, whether these are crests, capes, breast-shields or flank-feathers. Their dancing display, like that of blackcocks, is highly ritualised and formalised.

Greater Bird of Paradise

In this species, the female is plain, and dull brown in colour. The male is magnificent. The female builds her nest without the aid of the male, and rears the family by herself. The males are polygamous. Their only association with the females is when they are visited by them on the display ground.

Magnificent Bird of Paradise

This species is found in New Guinea. The males clear an area about 15 feet in diameter, and use this as a display ground while they await the females. Before and during the displaying season, the male displays in high branches and near the ground, spreading wide his brilliant cape, and puffing out his feathers.

Superb Bird of Paradise

The superb bird of paradise is found in the mountain forests of south eastern New Guinea. The male of this species displays in the trees, spreading wide his collar and breast-shield.

King Bird of Paradise

This is the smallest of the birds of paradise, found in the jungles of New Guinea, where it nests in trees. In the breeding season, the males perform their display in the highest trees.

Lyre Bird

The lyre birds are found in eastern Australia. There are two species, with many names. The one by which they are usually known – lyre bird – refers to the resemblance of their tail to the Greek lyre. This resemblance is not always obvious, but is noticeable when the birds are in full display. Other names for the lyre bird are Botany Bay pheasant and native pheasant. Lyre birds have been known to science only since 1798, when the first specimens were killed. They were at first thought to be members of the pheasant family, but they are not. The females build a nest of sticks, which is placed on the ground, or on a tree-stump or fork, sometimes on a rock ledge. The single chick is born blind and clothed in black down, which at once makes it different from all members of the pheasant family. Lyre birds are still fairly plentiful, and in certain parts of Australia become quite tame, due to the fact that they are protected and large numbers of people go to see them. This was not always the case. For a period of a century, the birds were ruthlessly slaughtered for their tail-feathers.

Fantail Flycatcher

The fantail flycatcher is found in Australia and Oriental regions. It is a member of a very large family of insect-eating birds, British representatives of which are the spotted flycatcher and the pied flycatcher.

Golden Whistler

The golden whistler is another flycatcher, found in Australia and neighbouring islands. Birds of this group are known by many names, whistlers and thickheads being two of them. In the present species, both sexes incubate the eggs, and both assist in rearing the young.

Blue Wren

The blue wren is one of ten species of Australian wrens, variously known as fairy wrens or superb warblers. These wrens have long tails and brilliant plumage.

Australian Robin

The Australian robin is one of a number of species with red breasts to which this name is applied, although it is strictly a member of the same family as the flycatchers.

Emperor Penguin

Emperor Penguin

Emperor penguins are flightless birds of Antarctica. They are the largest of this diverse family. The emperor stands about 3 feet tall and weighs up to 100 lbs. This makes it the world's largest and heaviest seabird.

Emperors breed only on the shores of the Antarctic. They breed in the coldest part of the winter, during the darkest period, and have to tend their chicks carefully to enable them to survive. The male emperor broods the single egg which he holds on his feet for a period of two months or more. During this time, the female penguins are out at sea. The penguin chicks hatch in July and August, and are fed by the male bird from secretions in his crop. When the chick is 5 or 6 weeks old, food becomes very abundant. It is then fed by both parents, and grows rapidly.

King Penguin

Adélie Penguin

Great Skua of Antarctica

King Penguin

The king penguin is a smaller bird than the emperor, weighing up to 40 lbs. All other species of penguin are much smaller than this. Unlike the emperor, where only the male incubates the egg, both sexes of the king penguin take turns and both help in rearing the single chick.

Adélie Penguin

The adélie penguin (above right) is much smaller. It builds a nest of stones, and lays 2 eggs. Male and female share the work of building. Two eggs are usual.

The incubation period is about thirty-five days. During the incubation period, the bird in charge of the egg fasts while the other hunts at sea. When the partner returns, the roles are reversed. Each fasting period lasts about a fortnight.

Great Skua of Antarctica

The great skua of Antarctica is a pirate on other species. It is also a predator on penguin eggs. This is the same species as the one found in Britain. In Shetland, it is known as the bonxie.

Glossary

Brooding: The act of a mother bird covering her young family.

Carnivorous: Flesh-eating.

Carrion: Any dead animal. A carrion eater is one which eats animals found dead.

Circumpolar: A circumpolar species is one found round the polar region of the world.

Coniferous: A coniferous forest is a forest of cone-bearing trees, e.g. pine, spruce.

Crop: The first compartment of a bird's digestive system, where the food goes before it passes on to the stomach.

Cycle: Some animal and bird species fluctuate in numbers over a regular period of years. This period is known as a cycle.

Eaglet: A young eagle.

Evolution: The gradual development and change of species over long periods of time.

Falconer: A person who trains hawks and falcons to hunt for him.

Gregarious: Living in groups, e.g. rooks.

Habitat: The place where any species finds living conditions to suit its needs.

Incubate: To sit on eggs until they hatch.

Insectivorous: Feeding on insects.

Invertebrate: Animals that have no bony skeleton, e.g. insects and worms.

Irruption: Applied to birds which appear in numbers in certain countries at irregular intervals, e.g. crossbills appearing in Britain.

Lek: Ceremonial display of the male black grouse.

Migrant: A bird which spends one season of the year in one part of the world, and the remainder of the year in another part.

Mimicry: The act of imitating.

Monogamous: A bird or animal which takes only one mate. Most of them will take a new mate if they lose the first.

Nectar: Fluid secreted by flowers, collected by humming birds and bees.

Nocturnal: Applied to species which are active only during the night.

Omnivorous: Literally a species which eats all things. Applied to species that eat both animal and vegetable food, usually in a great variety.

Pampas: The grassy plains of South America, akin to the North American prairies.

Passage Migrant: A migrant which is passing through any country on its way to breed or to winter in another country.

Pelagic: A pelagic bird is one which, outside the breeding season, spends all its time at sea.

Polygamous: A polygamous bird or animal is one which collects a harem, e.g. black grouse, red deer.

Prairie: The great grassy plains of North America are known as prairies.

Predator: Any species that kills other species for a living.

Promiscuous: Applied to species where the males mate with any female of the species.

Regurgitation: The act of disgorging food, applied to birds like wood pigeons and bullfinches which disgorge food for their chicks.

Scavenger: A species which devours carrion, offal and other waste matter.

Semi-desert: Dry regions of the world which are partly grassland, and not quite desert.

Territory: The area of ground defended by any species against its own kind or against competitive species. Its home area.

Tundra: The Arctic barren land which rings the world south of the polar ice cap.

Understorey: Term used to define the middle-growth in a forest, under the main tree canopy.

Vegetarian: Applies to species that eat only food of plant origin.

Index

93

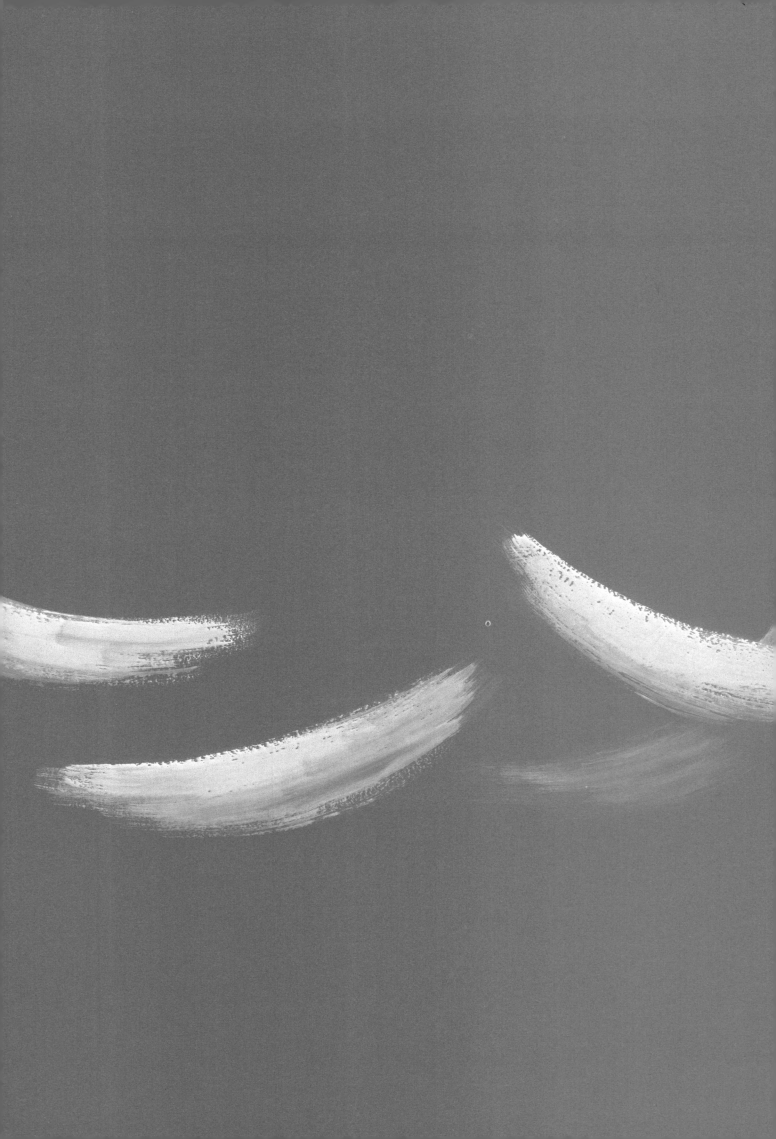